tadeusz Różewicz

Mother Departs

Mother Departs

by Tadeusz Różewicz

translated by Barbara Bogoczek

edited and introduced by Tony Howard

STORK
PRESS

Published by
Stork Press Ltd
170 Lymington Avenue
London
N22 6JG

www.storkpress.co.uk

English edition first published 2013 by Stork Press
1

Translated from the original *Matka odchodzi* © Tadeusz Różewicz, 1999
English translation © Barbara Bogoczek, 2013
Introduction © Tony Howard, 2013

This publication has been funded by
the Book Institute – the ©POLAND Translation Program

The publisher gratefully acknowledges assistance from the Polish Cultural
Institute in London for its support towards the publication of this book

Hardback 978-0-9573912-0-8
Paperback 978-0-9573912-1-5
eBook 978-0-9573912-2-2

Printed in the UK by MPG Books Group Ltd

introduction

AS THE MILLENNIUM APPROACHED, the great Polish poet Tadeusz Różewicz, who was born in 1921, contemplated the condition of a world that he felt had learned nothing from the violence of the twentieth century.

In a speech given in England after the fall of the Berlin Wall, he warned against indiscriminately jettisoning all values, all sense of justice and equity, and of casually burying 'rationalism and even [...] the Renaissance and the Reformation'.[1] Różewicz foresaw a 'return to religion [...] prompted by fear' and worst of all, as he warned in his long poem *recycling* from 1994, he saw recent history being either forgotten or denied: 'the Holocaust never happened/ now nobody can recall/ the weight of a human tear/ the price of tears is falling on the stock exchange/ panic in the market'.[2] He sensed new kinds of crises looming around the globe.

'My decimated generation,' he said, 'is now departed and dying, duped and disillusioned.' Out of this disillusionment Różewicz turned inwards in the 1990s. He examined his own family against the experiences of the twentieth century and, in 1999, he published *Mother Departs*. It is perhaps his most personal work. Certainly it is the work which a broad public has welcomed most warmly: it won the Nike Prize, Poland's most prestigious literary award; it was adapted as a theatre piece which toured internationally; it's an MP3 download. It touches a nerve.

In this book, Różewicz brings together writings by his mother Stefania, by his brothers and himself – memoirs, diaries, verses, short stories, pages from a notebook, torn letters, a single sentence on the back of a photograph. Looking back ('I am already older than you...'), he creates a kaleidoscopic portrait of his mother, of the times she lived in, and of her indelible influence on her three remarkable sons. The principal characters in this story are:

Stefania Maria Różewicz, née Gelbard (1896-1957)
Władysław Różewicz (1885-1977)

Their sons:
Janusz (*diminutives: Januszek, Jaś*) (1918-1944)
    Poet. Partisan with the underground Home Army; executed by the Gestapo

Tadeusz (*Tadziu, Tadzio*) (b. 1921)
    Poet, playwright. Partisan with the underground Home Army

Stanisław (*Staś, Stasiu*) (1924-2008)
    Film director

Tadeusz's wife:
Wiesława Różewicz, née Kozłowska
    Courier with the underground Home Army

Tadeusz and Wiesława's sons:
Kamil (b. 1950)
Jan (*Janek, Jaś*) (1953-2008)

Stefania Gelbard was born in 1896 in Lututów, a town eighty-five kilometres south-west of Łódź, or the 'Polish Manchester'. At the age of five she moved to Szynkielew (present-day population around three hundred) and it is life here that she describes in detail in the second chapter, 'The Village of my Childhood'. Tadeusz Drewnowski – in his study of Różewicz, *The Struggle for Breath* – writes that Stefania 'came from a Jewish family, the Gelbards. She ran away from home when she was young. From then until she married, she was raised and worked in the parish house of Father Michnikowski in Osjaków.'[3] Stefania was christened by Michnikowski, the long-serving parish priest for thirty-two villages in the district. In *Mother Departs* Tadeusz and Stanisław both recall childhood visits to his parish house.

Różewicz juxtaposes the chaotic and clamorous 'Now' of the 1990s with his mother's recollections of a distant rural world. Stefania gives an almost ethnographic account of the customs, beliefs and daily struggles of peasants, farmers and labourers living in a part of divided Poland that was still ruled by the Tsar and seemed blanketed by injustice and superstition: she brings the past to life with clarity, humour and often a sense of outrage. She is endlessly intrigued by the details and the rituals – courtship; marriage; the best way to put a spell on someone; clothing; diet; the ostentatious steward who used money as toilet paper; the dire consequences of building thatched wooden houses close together in a village with no fire brigade (Russia saw such local organisations as security threats). She presents childbirth as a battleground between midwives who might let a mother die in order to save the child (or rather its soul), and medics who would remove a trapped baby by crushing its skull and extracting the brain. 'The peasants were very accepting,' Stefania concludes: people often did not associate their situation with 'the times they lived in'. Stefania married Władysław Różewicz, a court clerk. They later moved to the small town of Radomsko, where Tadeusz was born.

She was intensely religious and, as a child, Tadeusz inherited this piety: 'As far as I can remember, my first poem was called "The Wooden Church",' published in his school magazine. It was a faith from which he would later detach himself, 'but of course the seeds of childhood remained: the devil, angels, the good Lord.'[4] Stefania writes that as a boy Tadeusz dreamed of being a farmer. The countryside in the 1920s and 1930s that he evokes seems almost unchanged from the Poland his mother described – carts still rumble down dirt tracks, farm workers regard trains and travel with suspicion – until 1939 when the fields, woods and rivers where the three brothers played during the summer holidays were violated.

Tadeusz had left school the previous year without taking his final baccalaureate examination, because his parents couldn't afford to keep him there. He worked as a clerk and a labourer and hoped to study forestry but his education was abruptly broken off by the invasion of Poland. Very close to what was then the German border, Radomsko fell quickly. It was occupied on 3rd September 1939, two days after the war began. Nazi planes bombed the Metalurgia factory, and Długa Street where the Różewicz family used to live. Columns of people fleeing into the countryside and the woods were machine-gunned from the air.

There is an all-pervasive sense of evil in Różewicz's writing. It is entirely man-made though: for him, God's failure to intervene casts a shadow over faith. Lututów, Osjaków and Radomsko all had thriving Jewish communities – Radomsko's numbered at least seven thousand in 1939. The Nazis created ghettos in all three places – Radomsko's was the second in Poland – brutally rounding up the local population. The names Gelbard and Gelbart appear in regional lists of the victims of the Holocaust. In the late summer of 1942 the programme to send the Jews to the camps began. In Osjaków, several hundred men, women and children were forced into the church, where they remained without food for days, before selection and transportation. Seventeen thousand people confined in the ghetto in the centre of Radomsko were sent to die in Treblinka. By the summer of 1943 the town was declared *Judenrein*: 'free of Jews'. Stefania and her family left Radomsko for Częstochowa days before their home was raided.

Tadeusz enlisted in the Home Army in 1941 (*Armia krajowa*: the A. K.) and in 1943 he joined the partisan fighters – 'in the woods', as people said. He edited his unit's newsletter and his commander encouraged him to channel the resistance's experiences into literature. In 1944, helped by his future wife Wiesława who was a courier for the underground, he mimeographed and circulated one hundred copies of *Forest Echoes*, a collection of verse and prose including work by his elder brother. Janusz Różewicz was a promising published poet. He had trained as an army officer just before the invasion and then worked in the underground military intelligence (codenames: Gustaw, Zbyszek). He was betrayed to the Gestapo, tortured, and was shot in the Jewish cemetery in Łódź in November 1944. 'How my poor mother suffered all those years after Janusz's death,' Tadeusz wrote in his diary in 1957, 'right until today – this very day. I cannot think about what the Gestapo did to him.' Stefania wrote on the back of a photograph: 'year 1944 cruel to me'. Janusz haunts *Mother Departs*: his execution, its unspoken effects on the family, and later the ugly, unjust inevitability of Stefania's own death from cancer in a sweltering industrial city in People's Poland – these are at the core of this book.

When the war ended, Tadeusz studied art history in Kraków, where he encountered many established and emerging writers, painters and filmmakers, and he began to contribute to literary journals: 'I was full of worshipful admiration for works of art (the aesthetic experience having replaced the religious), but at the same time, there grew within me a contempt for all aesthetic values.'[5] He was determined to confront the brutality of the war and the sanctioned inhumanity that seemed to have devalued everything, including words themselves:

waiting for me at home
a task:
Create poetry after Auschwitz [6]

It was a responsibility which he saw as generational rather than private. He wrote for survivors: 'We learnt language from scratch, these people and I.' Comparing many writers to butterfly collectors, catching and displaying pretty phrases, 'I consciously gave up the privileges that accrue to poetry [...] and I turned to the banal truth, to common sense [...] I returned to my rubbish heap.'[7] In 1947 his groundbreaking volume *Anxiety* (*Niepokój*) appeared and his stark, stripped, brutally honest poetry, distrustful of any trace of rhetoric or pretence, became one of the key moral voices of post-war literature.

His work was profoundly controversial: it attracted the support of the veteran Polish poet Leopold Staff (1878-1957) who became a mentor and friend, but Różewicz alienated both traditionalists and the new Marxist orthodoxy with the un-idealised frankness of his writing. 'I bought two volumes by Różewicz, and I burned both of them,' said the poet Jan Bolesław Ożóg in *Życie literackie* (1954) in a group discussion of Różewicz's work. Such literary round tables, Czesław Miłosz wrote in *The Captive Mind*, were 'a sort of trial'.[8] Some of Różewicz's writing tried to be as affirmative as the Party wanted. The poem 'It was January' celebrated some Russian soldiers who came to the house 'in the bright of day' and 'helped mother', but at a young writers' assembly in 1948 Różewicz mocked the Marxist journal *Kuźnica* for trying to impose doctrinaire thinking on the content and form of Polish writing and for encouraging opportunists. He derided what became known as the *pryszczaci*, the 'pimpled' generation of young literary Stalinists. In 1949 Socialist Realism was declared the official literary mode at the Congress of Polish Writers' Union; formal experimentation was condemned, and Różewicz was denounced in his absence by the poet Wiktor Woroszylski for 'succumbing to the influence of bourgeois literature'.

That year Tadeusz and Wiesława moved to the industrial city of Gliwice in Silesia, far from all the careerist literary circles and as far as possible from involvement with shifts in Party power and dogma. The attacks on Różewicz's 'catastrophism' and negativity continued, taken up by the circle around *Kuźnica* and the influential weekly *Nowa Kultura,* whose editor-in-chief from 1950-52 was Wiktor Woroszylski. Looking back at these years in the 1957 'Gliwice Diary' section of *Mother Departs,* Różewicz recalls the problems he faced getting his work published between 1948 and 1955 – and especially between 1950 and 1953 when he was 'treated like a piece of rubbish' and *Nowa Kultura* rejected 'Regarding a Certain Incident (A Polemical Poem 1953)' as 'nihilistic' and unprintable.

This period was in his mind during the long oppressive summer of 1957 when both Stefania and Leopold Staff died. Polish cultural and political life was now in a state of upheaval following Khruschev's denunciation of Stalin's crimes, and the Hungarian Uprising. Adam Ważyk, the founder of *Kuźnica,* caused a sensation in 1955 with 'A Poem for Adults' in *Nowa Kultura,* in which he denounced the Stalinism he had imposed for a decade. The editorial staff was purged – and Wiktor Woroszylski returned as editor-in-chief. But after the 'Polish October' of 1956, when workers' protests led to Władysław Gomułka becoming the leader of a 'liberalising' government, Woroszylski himself broke with Moscow over Hungary. Różewicz found the literary cliques' rapid reinventions of themselves repellent and in the diary he calls Woroszylski a 'cynic'. But at the same time he experienced a crisis in his own writing.

Różewicz was struggling with a sense of his poetry's redundancy, trying to force himself to write prose that might document reality truthfully, and as his mother's illness worsened, the diary recorded his reading: Flaubert; the Polish novelists Henryk Sienkiewicz and Bolesław Prus; Camus and Céline. He once told his translator Adam Czerniawski, 'I search books and poems for practical help. I hope they will help me overcome despair and doubt.' Even at the beginning of *Mother Departs*, we find Różewicz arguing with Cyprian Norwid (1821-1883), the precursor of modern Polish poetry. And yet inevitably all this 'led to disappointment – after all, these were only books'.[9]

In the summer of 1957 Różewicz had just returned from Paris, his first visit to the West, which was permitted because of growing acclaim for his work. But as he reveals in the book *Our Elder Brother*, this was a disturbing experience. In 1943, the last time they saw each other, he and Janusz swore that if they survived but lost touch they would meet again in Paris. Tadeusz wrote in March 1957: 'I am looking at this city as if... as if I ended up here after death... In my indifference there is something unnatural or perhaps... I am simply dead.' He recorded a meeting with another Polish poet in Paris, 'Czesław M.,' who told him, '"Looking at you, I worry for Polish poetry... it's as if you didn't care for anything... You do not see Paris." He said it with care, with compassion, he spoke to me like an Elder Brother.' In the 'Gliwice Diary', all Tadeusz can bring back with him from France are the harsh visions of Camus and Céline and the embryo of a poem: 'The Seine doesn't exist. There's only... There's no Eiffel Tower. There's no Paris. There's a mouth.'[10]

Yet in this state of traumatic depression and with Stefania dying despite everything faith and medicine could do for her, Różewicz was also thinking about contemporaries whom he cherished for their integrity. They include Staff; Henryk Vogler (here 'Henryk V'), a Jewish camp survivor who became head of the publishing house Wydawnictwo Literackie; and Kornel Filipowicz ('Kornel'), whose story about the life of three survivors in the post-war years Różewicz had developed as a screenplay, entitled *Three Women* (1956). His younger brother Stanisław directed it and, if Janusz Różewicz is a key figure in *Mother Departs* because of his tragic absence, Stanisław is also crucial to this book. In 1961 he and Tadeusz co-wrote the film *Birth Certificate*, which won prizes in Venice and Cannes. It presents the Occupation from the point of view of children – including one plot that deals with the relationship of three brothers and their mother, and another with Mirka, a young Jewish girl passing as a Christian: 'It is all about shaking off, getting rid of the psychological burden which the war was,' Stanisław said, 'we share many war memories'.[11]

In the months following Stefania's death, Tadeusz Różewicz began to construct another identity, as a playwright, and in dramas such as *The Card Index* he developed his surreal collage style – a democratic form where many voices compete and overlap and there is no one definitive truth to discover. Both his theatre and film work were collaborative, of course, and when, years later in *Mother Departs,* Różewicz applies similar principles to reconstructing the lives of his family and himself, he creates a montage of memories. We frequently see the same moments through different eyes – a country holiday; reading a magazine on the floor; snow, birds and bailiffs bursting into the family's kitchen; the deaths of two aviators, national heroes. The flow of history is experienced in snapshots; facts are redrafted as fictions or stripped down into a set of ferociously honest poems by Różewicz himself. Most of these date from the immediate post-war years and the first, 'Hands in Shackles', written earlier still, is retrieved from his clandestine first volume *Forest Echoes*. We are challenged as readers to put it all into some order, to discover resonances and meanings of our own.

Tadeusz gives the last words to his two brothers: suddenly their childhood becomes an urban one and Stefania, chatting about film stars and dealing with teachers, is a different person. The lighter tone is supported by their father, too, whom Tadeusz takes longer to appreciate or understand, but whose voice is heard in several poems addressed to him. In one not included in *Mother Departs*, 'Things Fell into Place', the ageing poet makes his way to Władysław's grave at Częstochowa, passing 'Henryk's tomb' and 'Aunt Helen's' and 'Uncle Józef's'. And – 'things fell into place'. Touching the gravestone, he remembers that his father once told him to write more like the nineteenth-century novelists: 'your little volumes are so slim'.[12] *Mother Departs* is an elegy, a tribute, and a painfully raw investigation into the emotional bonds between parent and child. It is still a slim book, but his family collaborate with him to give it the breadth and depth and intricacy of life.

[Note: this translation follows the sometimes unconventional punctuation and capitalisation of Różewicz's text.]

1 Tadeusz Różewicz, 'Humanity's Footprint', translated by Adam Czerniawski, *Poetry Review* 81 (3), 1991, p. 27.

2 Różewicz, *recycling,* translated by Barbara Bogoczek and Tony Howard (Todmorden: Arc Press, 2001), p. 43.

3 Tadeusz Drewnowski, *Walka o oddech: O pisarstwie Tadeusza Różewicza* (Warsaw: Wydawnictwo Artystyczne i Filmowe, 1990), p. 38.

4 'Tadeusz Różewicz in Conversation with Adam Czerniawski', *The New Review* (25), 1976, p. 10.

5 Różewicz, *The Survivor and Other Poems*, translated by Magnus J. Krynski and Robert A. Maguire (Princeton: Princeton University Press, 1976), p. xi.

6 Różewicz, *Poezja 2* (Kraków: Wydawnictwo Literackie, 1988), p. 344.

7 Różewicz, *The Survivor*, p. xvii.

8 Czesław Miłosz, *The Captive Mind* (London: Heinemann, 1960), p. 190.

9 'Tadeusz Różewicz in Conversation with Adam Czerniawski', p. 16.

10 The fullest account of these events, especially those relating to Janusz's career and death, appears in Tadeusz Różewicz, *Nasz Starszy Brat* (Wrocław: Wydawnictwo Dolnośląskie, 1992), the first of the investigations into family history and memory to which he turned in the last decade of the

twentieth century. The events of the Holocaust in the region continue to be researched and documented. For Lututów, Osjaków and Radomsko, for example, see *The United States Holocaust Memorial Museum Encyclopaedia of Camps and Ghettoes 1933-1945,* vol. 2 (Bloomington: Indiana University Press, 2012) pp. 83-85, 293-295.

11 Quoted in the booklet accompanying *50th Anniversary of The Polish Film School*, DVD, 2007.

12 Różewicz, *They Came to See a Poet*, translated by Adam Czerniawski (London: Anvil Press, 1991), pp. 216-7.

Mother's eyes rest on me

now

NOW, as I write these words, my mother's eyes rest on me. The eyes, mindful and tender, are silently asking, 'what's troubling you, my darling...?' With a smile I reply, 'nothing... everything's fine Mummy, really,' 'but tell me,' Mother says, 'what's the matter?' I turn my head away, look through the window...

Mother's eyes which can see everything watch the birth watch throughout life and watch after death from the 'other world'. Even if they turned her son into a killing machine or a beast a murderer mother's eyes are looking at him with love... looking.

When a mother turns her eyes away, her child starts to stray, becomes lost in a world stripped of love and warmth.

Tomorrow's Mother's Day. I don't remember if when I was a child there was an official day like that... When I was a child every day was Mother's day. Every morning Mother's day. And noon and evening and night.

You know Mummy, I can tell it only to you in my old age, and I can tell you now because I'm already older than you... I didn't dare tell you when you were alive. I'm a Poet. It's a word that frightened me, I never spoke it to Father... I didn't know if it was decent to say something like that.

I entered the world of poetry as if into the light and now I'm preparing to exit, into darkness... I trekked across the landscape of poetry and have seen it with the eye of a fish a mole a bird a child a grown man and an old man; why is it so difficult to utter these words: 'I'm a poet', you search for synonyms to help you come out to the world. To Mother. Of course, Mother knows. But to say something like that to my father was unthinkable... So I never did tell Father 'Dad... Father... I'm a poet'. I don't know if my father would even have noticed... he'd be so remote... he'd have said (while he read the paper, ate, dressed, polished his shoes...) 'what's that you're saying (Tadziu)?' After all it was just silly 'what's that again?' but of course I couldn't repeat it, let alone louder, 'Dad, Father, I am a poet'... Father might have looked up from his plate, his paper... looking surprised or perhaps not looking but nodding and saying 'good... good' or saying nothing at all. I wrote a poem called 'Father' (in 1954) 'Walking through my heart goes/ my old father...' I never knew if Father read that poem, he never said a word... anyway I never read it to Father either... now it's 1999... and my voice is so quiet that my Parents can't hear my words 'Mum, Dad, I'm a poet'... 'I know, Darling' Mother says 'I've always known.' 'Speak up' says Father 'I can't hear a thing'...

a poet's promises

For years I used to promise my Mum three things: that I'd invite her to Kraków, that I'd show her Zakopane and the mountains, that I'd take her to the seaside. Mum never got to see Kraków. She got to see neither Kraków nor the mountains (with Lake Morskie Oko in the middle) nor the sea. I didn't keep my promises... It's been nearly half a century since Mum's death... (anyway, clocks, calendars, I'm losing interest). Why didn't I take her to Kraków and show her the Sukiennice, Saint Mary's Church, Wawel Castle, the Vistula.

Oh yes. Her son lived in Kraków... and the young 'promising' poet... a poet who wrote so many poems for his mother and so many poems for all mothers... didn't bring Mum to Kraków not in 1947 nor 1949... She never insisted, never reproached me.

Mum never saw Warsaw. Mum never flew in an aeroplane, sailed on a ship. I never went with Mum to a café, restaurant, florist, theatre, opera... Or a concert... I was a poet... I wrote a poem 'A Tale of Old Women', I wrote a poem 'An Old Peasant Woman Walks Along The Beach'... I didn't take Mum to the seaside... I didn't sit with her on the beach, I didn't bring her a seashell or a bit of amber. Nothing... and she never will see the sea... and I'll never see her face and eyes and smile as she looks at the sea... a poet. Is a poet a man who writes lamentations dry-eyed, so that he can see the form clearly? Who must put all his heart into making sure the form's 'perfect'...? A poet: a man without a heart? And now the wailing in front of an audience at a book fair, the poetic indulgences, the Literary Stock Exchange. I can't even fool myself that 'in the other world' Mum is strolling through the Planty Gardens, through Kraków, to Wawel... Is there a beach in 'heaven' where our Mothers can sit in their poor old fur stoles, coats, slippers and hats...? But even now I'm writing – dry-eyed – and 'correcting' these beggarly lamentations of mine...

in the midst of life

It is now sixty years since World War II broke out.

I'm 77, 78 years old. I am a poet. At the start of the road I couldn't believe in the miracle... that one day I'd become a poet, sometimes at night woken by nightmares and spectres I clutched at the thought 'I shall be a poet' I shall drive away spectres darkness death... I shall enter the light of poetry, the music of poetry, the Silence.

Now as I write these words, Mother's quiet mindful eyes are on me. She watches me from the 'other world' the other side I do not believe in. In this world another war is raging. One of the hundred that have raged continuously from the end of World War II until today...

My world that I tried to build for half a century is crumbling into fragments under the rubble of houses hospitals and temples man and god are dying, man and hope are dying, man and love.

Once, a long time ago in 1955, I wrote a poem 'In the Midst of Life'...

After the end of the world
after death
I found myself in the midst of life
creating myself
building life
people animals landscapes

this is a table I said
this is a table
on the table there is bread a knife
the knife is for cutting the bread
bread feeds people
man must be loved
I was learning night and day
what must be loved
man I answered

a poet! He grew old he stands on death's doorstep and still he hasn't understood that a knife is for hacking heads off hacking off noses and ears what is a knife for? for cutting heads off... some place over there, far? near? what else is a knife for? for cutting out tongues that speak in foreign tongues and for cutting open the bellies of pregnant women cutting off the breasts of nursing mothers cutting off genitals gouging out eyes... and what else can we look at on television? read in the papers? hear on the radio?

what is a knife for
it's for cutting off the heads of enemies
it's for cutting off the heads of
women children old people
(That's what they've been writing in the papers
for a century...)

now as I write these words mother's quiet eyes are on me
on my hand on these maimed blinded words.
our mothers' eyes that penetrate hearts and thoughts are our
conscience they judge us and love
full of love and anxiety
mother's eyes
Mother watches her son as he takes his first steps and then as
he seeks his way, her eyes watch as the son leaves, they take in
the whole life and death of her son

possibly my words will reach mothers who abandoned their
children on a rubbish dump or reach children who have forgotten
their parents in the hospitals and the old people's homes

I remember Mother saying
to us, only once probably... I was five... only once in her life
she said to us 'I shall leave you... you're so naughty... I shall
go and won't ever
come back'... three small naughty boys... I have remembered
all through my
life the fear and dark despair that we three felt...
I remember my heart bleeding (oh yes 'my heart was bleeding')
I found myself in emptiness and darkness... Mum only said
it once
and today I still remember my tears and despair...
but mum didn't go away she was with us and she will be...
now as I write these words... mother's searching eyes are on me

I lift my head, open my eyes... can't find my way, fall, get up, words filled with hatred ptomaine explode rip love faith and hope apart... I open my mouth to say something 'people must be loved' not Poles Germans Serbs Albanians Italians Jews Greeks... people must be loved... white black red yellow

I know my beggarly wailings lack good taste...

and I know that of all worldly things what survives is... what?!

The great ludicrous genius Norwid said:

Of all worldly things only two survive,
Two only: poetry and goodness... and nothing else...

Oh Don Quixote, it's the Nothing that's survived! And if we do not begin to use our heads at last, do not get some grip on this vast expanding Nothing, then... then what? speak up, don't look so petrified! what's about to happen... we shall make such a hell on earth for ourselves that Lucifer will look like an angel, oh a fallen angel yes but not absolutely without a soul, prone to hubris yet at least dense with longing for a lost heaven dense with melancholy with sorrow... and politics will turn into kitsch, love into pornography, music into pandemonium, sport into prostitution, religion into science, science into faith.

the village of my childhood

Stefania Różewicz

IN THE TSAR'S DAY the village of Szynkielew belonged to the *guberniya* of Kalisz, the *poviat* of Wieluń.

There are two manors: the local gentry's and the Governor-General's. The village itself is large. Although not as poor as other nearby villages, there is a great deal of poverty here. The roads are terrible. In the winter, if the ground has not frozen, clogs literally vanish into the mud, because a leg can't hang on to a clog while you're dragging yourself out of the mud. The clogs have wooden soles. Hardly anyone has proper shoes, they are a luxury. Those who do will only wear them for special occasions. There is no school, to reach church people have to walk nine kilometres.

I came to Szynkielew when I was five. I really liked it tremendously. I did not understand how so much human poverty could hide behind the beauty of nature, even in a better-off village like this. When I was about ten I began to notice the life of the common people. From those times I best remember the year 1905. Folk from town came and told us the Tsar would soon be gone, that the people in Łódź had made an effigy and dressed it up like the Tsar. They paraded it around to mock him. Another day I heard that people had boiled a cook. And that happened in the army, so there was hope the Tsar would go and people wouldn't be taken away to Siberia any more.

The village was horribly neglected. The rulers made no effort at all to improve people's condition. The best proof is that one tiny school was supposed to suffice for several villages in the area. So children scarcely ever went to school, because in winter when there was so much snow it was impossible for them to get through, and then in spring and autumn the parents couldn't allow children to waste their time, as they put it, because one child had to look after another. I saw it for myself when three- or four-year-old children had to feed toddlers and babies and keep them quiet while the mothers weren't home. The mortality rate among the children was high. The strongest survived, but as for the frail ones – there was no one to treat them, no nourishment for them.

I remember visiting some farming people once who were quite well off. The mother was in the field. There was a baby left at home lying in a cradle in bare straw. The straw might have been covered with some sort of cloth but the baby had kicked it away. It was a sorry sight, the baby had defecated and started eating the faeces. Hygiene was appalling. Children went to bed at night without washing. They were exhausted, because a child who was five or six already had to mind the geese. The children never got enough sleep. I often saw tiny infants dragged from their beds to mind the cows or geese at four or five in the morning, they would fall asleep on the edge of some field while the animals wandered off. My God, I was so sorry for the children whose cows or geese strayed, and the poor little cowherds were scared in case the cattle might cause damage. They chased them, tried to bring them in, and if they couldn't, they'd get a beating at home for failing to mind the livestock.

Children were undernourished. Very often there was no bread. Then the mother would hurriedly make a pie from potato scraps and some flour and bake it on the stove or the cinders. It was a great day when a child got a bit of a bun or a sweet. The sweet would be the worst kind. The colouring was made from starch, with saccharin not sugar.

I had a chance to observe the dreadful existence of the smallholders. Those who never saw it first-hand wouldn't believe it. A smallholder had three or four acres of land, sometimes just sandy soil (and many only had two or three acres), and lots of children. Sometimes there was an old granny too on what they called a 'life tenancy.' I remember I went into one of their rooms once; there were no floorboards, just compacted clay – one space housing a family and the rabbits they reared for meat at Christmas. The window was tiny, nailed up so you couldn't open it. The better-off had different windows, with four panes. All the roofs were straw.

Smallholders couldn't afford to keep a work horse, so they had to labour for the better-off who later helped them transport their manure in return, sometimes corn. The rich always brought in their own harvest first, while the poor man's grain got drenched. In the autumn the rich farmers would already be ploughing and sowing while the poor man – who had to work to pay off his debts – still had his rye in the field. When the first frost came I often saw smallholders carrying their harvest on their backs into some dilapidated shed. And this was usually the women, because their men would have gone away to work in Germany, to earn some extra money and buy shoes or clothes. Even the better-off farmers had to send their children to Germany to work. Nobody could clothe themselves from what farming earned.

The homes were very poorly furnished. Usually there was not much more than a box, they called it a chest, containing clothes and linen. The linen was very modest; shirts had three sections: it was thick cloth at the bottom like a sack, higher up the cotton was thinner, and at the very top the collar was made from fine cotton bought in a shop. As for the bed covers, underneath it was homespun cloth, on top it was patchwork squares.

There were no mattresses. You could say people lay in bare straw, usually several slept in one bed. There might be sheets thrown over the straw, but they would kick them off in their sleep. Better-off people had tables, but they usually ate on benches. They put small stools beside the bench, that's how

*Mum after graduating from the housekeeping course
at the Kozarski manor house in Konopnica*

they sat for a meal. They ate from quite large bowls, so for a family of six or five the housewife would lay out two bowls of food.

There were hardly any dishes in the kitchen, perhaps two or three iron pots which they called *żeleźniaki*. Some housewives had a few plates but kept them in the cupboard for show. I never saw a proper washing bowl. There was a big wooden tub where they did the washing up and they used the same tub for watering cows. With my own eyes I saw little children get up in the morning and pee in it too. Some people washed themselves by sucking up water and spitting onto their hands. Still others washed themselves in a *szkopek*. That was for milking cows. Everybody ate together from one or two clay bowls.

Normally food in the village was equally poor. Breakfast usually meant potatoes and *polewka,* which was a kind of sauce. It could be made several ways. Poor people thickened water with rye flour, sour milk, richer people used fresh milk, and buttermilk instead of water. In the countryside potatoes were usually cooked in their skins. Dinner probably meant potatoes, cabbage and dumplings, of which there were a variety. Sometimes they had *zacierka,* small dumplings with milk, or bigger ones called *bociany* (storks), with buttermilk. The cabbage was pickled whole and the loose leaves were chopped and shredded and mixed with the cabbage heads. Poor households enriched the cabbage with some oil or cooked beans. Millet or pearl barley were common too. Those were usually cooked in the days before the harvest when food was scarce. They hardly ever ate meat. If a cow broke her leg or there was some other accident the peasants would share the meat among themselves, but generally a butcher would come and buy it for a pittance. When the rye yielded a good harvest, those were the happy times. They would bake white bread for every Sunday. But when the crop was bad the women could only grind rye in the quern to make soups and sauces, borscht and other *polewki*. They hardly ever ate sugar and only bought it for religious festivals or for the sick.

As for vegetables, in the old days people didn't grow them. I never saw red carrots, only the white sort they used for animal fodder. There were no vegetables in the village, I clearly recall that, because women always came to us for green parsley as medicine for their new babies. If a baby couldn't pass urine, they made a parsley infusion as a diuretic and gave it to the baby to drink. Fruit was no better. It was mostly wild pears. They grew between the fields, and so thickly that it looked like a wood from a distance. This wild fruit was abundant but I'm sure the pears couldn't provide many vitamins because they were so very hard. There were two orchards in the village with good quality fruit. They belonged to the manor house and were leased out to some Jews; the fruit didn't benefit the village children. But yes, I do remember a few small gardens owned by rich farmers too.

The village was large, and wealthy compared to other hamlets, but there was literally not one single family who could afford to send their child – not even a gifted one – off to school in the town. I knew a few boys who had the potential, but they had to go to Germany and work. Against all the odds, there were two in my generation who wanted to make something of themselves as people used to say, and so one of them – Andrzej Kałużny – went back and forth to Germany to save up for his education, or for clothes. Then he had to run nine kilometres to the parish priest, who was preparing him for school – Year Three or Four, I can't remember. Anyway he went to a seminary from which he returned utterly exhausted. People told me that at his *prymicja*, the first Mass, he had to be helped to the altar, he wasn't strong enough to celebrate Mass by himself any more. Soon afterwards he died.

The other boy was Antoni Walasik. He must have been very gifted, he had so many talents. More than once I saw him carving religious figures out of pine bark, really well. He was self-taught. His parents wouldn't even give him the money to buy a slate pencil and tablet, but he truly wanted to write so he did it with charcoal or sticks in the ground, and when he got older he used to trek to Germany to study writing. He wrote letters home for his fellow workers in Germany. Very few villagers could write. Almost everyone was illiterate. I must say more about Walasik because then he started to study by himself. After some years he stopped going to Germany, and the court secretary Mr Świerszczak took him in as a helper, to give him some experience. And although he was self-taught he managed very well. His handwriting was beautiful. He was so hard working. After this apprenticeship he went to Kalisz as a clerk.

I am describing these two people whom I knew to help readers realise what living conditions were like for folk who really had so much to offer to the culture and the community. Today, when I see hundreds of thousands of young people from rural areas gaining an education, I feel so happy that things have gone this way and aren't as they used to be in those tragic times for education, when I was young. I cannot stop thinking about my village where I grew up, about how it was then and how it is now. If someone in the village could write, even badly, then this scholar would gather the children in the winter and teach them too. He would get a few pennies or something in kind. Yet whatever the children learned in the winter, they would forget in the summer. Because in the summer this teacher went to work in the fields, and the children minded geese and cows.

To tell the truth, people didn't want schools. Because there was no education, ninety per cent would say their granddad or their great-granddad didn't know how to write, and he managed to survive without it – even if a few farmers wanted their children in a school, and even if they tried to persuade the authorities to start a school in the village. Sometimes Father would say, 'Your children badly need a school.' They would answer jokingly, 'He who knows how to write well, knows the right road to Hell.'

The village was deeply religious. Even the priest was treated like a saint. The poorest folk, who often denied themselves a piece of bread, found the rouble for the collection plate. Though the church was nine kilometres from the village, people went there every Sunday. In winter it was often bitterly cold, even so folk rose at four in the morning to go to Advent Mass. They strictly observed fasting. Lent before Easter and Advent before Christmas. Even so, if someone wanted to eat a slice of meat on a Sunday in Lent, they would go to the priest and ask for a dispensation. A dispensation cost a rouble. Throughout Lent, people virtually lived on *kapuśnica*, which was cabbage soup cooked with dried mushrooms or added oil. And there was fasting on the so-called 'cross days' (when there were penitential processions) and before every festival of the Virgin Mary. People belonged to all kinds of religious societies such as the 'Rosary Brotherhood'. The Rosary Brotherhood guaranteed that when you died, even if nobody paid, there would still be a mass and lots of candles at your funeral. There were many such societies, like the 'Circle for the Living Rosary', which meant that the women who were members gathered each Sunday at a different woman's place to say the Rosary. They said it was Living because they kept reciting it.

A baby was christened by two weeks at the latest. They were rightly afraid of the baby dying before it happened, because he or she would be condemned for eternity 'like a Jew' or some other un-christened person. The mother also had to go to church after childbirth, to be purified. Until then such a woman was not allowed to fetch any water because they said worms would appear in it. People went to confession quite often, and at Easter everybody had to undergo a special confession supervised by the parish priest. So someone from every house went to the parish office and bought a card for every member of the household, and then each person went to the confession with those cards. After confession they gave their card to the organist, and he would cross out the name in a book which included a list of all the people, this was compiled before Easter. And so the parish priest knew how many infidels he had. In my days few couples lived out of wedlock. Of course there were always a few cases in a parish.

I was talking about the Easter confession, I must also describe how Easter was celebrated out in the country. All Holy Week was rather solemn and sad. The parents went to Lent service and they told stories about Jews tormenting Jesus Christ, the earth splitting and thunderbolts crashing down. During the storytelling people took their hats off to show greater respect. Then the traditional spring-cleaning took place: whitewashing homes, washing the linen. Next came the baking of bread, richer people baked pies. You had to prepare your best Easter food to be blessed. On Holy Saturday the priest arrived to give the blessing. Women and children dressed up in Sunday clothes brought their Easter food to the front of the chapel. They sat in rows on the ground, which was sprinkled with yellow sand. The Easter food consisted of bread, cheese and *szperka*. *Szperka* is meat cooked with pork fat seasoned with bilberries. Vinegar and horseradish were essential. Vinegar because the Jews gave it to Jesus to drink. Nearly every adult went to the Resurrection Mass.

Holy Sunday was celebrated grandly. Easter Monday was all about *śmingus* – the traditional custom of drenching people with water. The farmboys drenched girls with hand pumps, and some girls ended up swimming in a ditch. Young men also went round the village with a *gaik*. This was a small Christmas tree decorated with various dollies and cockerels. While doing this they were singing, 'We've got the *gaik,* there's a chicken with an egg,' and the housewives would bring out a treat – a *dyngus* – which included eggs and a bit of pie or bread.

Christmas was a huge festival. People observed it reverently. There were very many dishes at Christmas Eve supper. You had to grind hemp grain and boil it with milk. That was Christmas Eve soup. There were honey dumplings, dried snow pears and many other treats. Christmas Eve supper consisted of seven, eleven or thirteen dishes. After sharing the holy wafer, the man of the house took a pink wafer (the church organist baked it specially) and he was allowed to give it to the cattle, because the peasants used to say, 'You must give some to the cattle, 'cos Lord Jesus come into this world among the cattle.' The villagers also said, 'The night Baby Jesus was born, the cattle spoke in the human language and even now the cattle talk on Christmas Eve.'

In a corner of the room they placed a sheaf of straw, and the whole chamber was lined with straw to commemorate the fact that Baby Jesus was born in a stable. On the Second Day of Christmas, named after St Stephen, the farmers swapped places with their farmhands and shepherds, hence the saying 'On St Stephen's Day every servant's a master.'

Then the carnival began. If a man had his eye on a girl, he would collect some vodka, choose a neighbour to be his *starost*, his wedding planner, and go matchmaking. If they struck a deal – that is, if the girl's parents offered as much land as the chap wanted (and if he already had land, he would accept money or cows) plus some extra arrangements on the side – they would all drink the vodka and have the banns published. If there was no deal, then on the very same night this chap and his *starost* would go round other girls until somebody said yes. Then they went to the parish priest. They asked him to read the banns. The priest would test to see if they knew their prayers. Very often the couple did not know their prayers. If so, the priest wouldn't read the banns until they had learned their prayers.

In fact the priest told them off: 'You know how to do certain other things, only you can't say your prayers.' The priest was right. The wedding took place after the property matters had been completed, and the church business.

The wedding was given by the parents on both sides. Usually the groom bought the vodka, paid for the music, paid the priest, and bought shoes for the bride. The bride would buy fabric for his wedding shirt, which she would sew herself. The wedding lasted several days. The outfits were colourful. The groom's best men spent the whole previous night going round and inviting guests. Almost everyone went. The best men were rather festively dressed. They all tossed scarves over their shoulders and wore caps decorated with flowers they'd bought, usually red flowers. They made themselves walking sticks, though I couldn't say which type of wood. I think it must have been willow because the sticks were stripped of bark. Later they carved the sticks with a knife and dyed them different colours. Every best man had to have a stick. The bridesmaids had coloured garlands of flowers on their heads, with long ribbons at the back reaching to the ground. It all looked pretty. The bride had a different headdress or a very flimsy veil. Only a virgin could wear a veil with a garland of mint. If the priest discovered the bride was pregnant or even had a child, he would rip the garland off her head in the church, because she was not a virgin and was unfit to marry in a garland. It was a warning to the rest to guard their maidenheads well, and it was shameful.

Sometimes, if the family was wealthier, as many as twenty carts went to the wedding. The horses wore flowery plumage. Before they set out, the young couple would thank their parents for their upbringing. There would be somebody who could read, so he would read about the state of wedlock, about Original Sin, about Adam and Eve as the first parents whom God Himself joined together at the beginning of the world. The

couple would kneel at their parents' feet before leaving to ask
for a blessing. They would set off for the wedding accompanied
by the singing of the bridesmaids and the groom's men – who
might also shoot off salutes. They played mournful music on
the way to the wedding. Usually the bride cried, bidding her
parents farewell. She also said farewell to her doorstep, as
follows:

> farewell my footpath,
> farewell my doorstep,
> here my feet learned their steps,
> alas no more, etc.

After the ceremony the entire wedding party went to the
inn. Everyone drank and danced. When they'd had enough of
a good time and were all drunk, they raced each other to the
wedding house. On the one hand this journey was extremely
jolly, with cheerful music, on the other hand the race often
ended with the carts upside down. When she returned from
the ceremony, the bride was led into the wedding house to
the accompaniment of wedding songs. What followed was
the bridal dinner and the *oczepowiny* – a ceremony where
the groom had to take the garland off the bride's head. The
bridesmaids would have done a supernatural job of attaching
it earlier so that removing it was like cutting the Gordian knot.
While this went on, everybody sang and drank vodka. The
bridesmaids sang wistful songs about losing your virginity,
and the *starost*'s wife circulated with vodka and a sieve. She
collected money in that for a new bonnet for the bride and
sang, 'Give her money for some pearls, so she can have pretty
girls.' The *starost* sang in response, 'Give her money for amber
toys, so she can have pretty boys, give her money for the sieve,
she'll have all she needs to live.' Through it all the bride sat on
the kneading trough. When the groom finally got her garland

off, the *starost*'s wife put the new bonnet on the bride's head. The bride took it off again, she placed it on her lap, because other housewives were also giving her bonnets, including her mother and mother-in-law. If she were wealthy she might collect twenty or so bonnets and perhaps a hundred roubles. The money set the couple up. The bonnets in our area were very pretty. Large, decorated with many colourful ribbons. Women wore beautiful silk scarves on top of the bonnet. On the second day the wedding party moved to the groom's parents, and on the third day they celebrated at the *starosts*'. Then the guests chipped in together. The men chipped in for the vodka, the women brought cheese, butter, eggs, sausage or even a freshly killed rabbit, and they resumed the eating, drinking, dancing, singing and playing all the way through until Sunday. Because weddings were usually on Tuesdays. On Sunday the bride would go to church for a blessing. The priest blessed the bride as a future mother.

Rich farmers often invited priests and the county clerk. The best guests were served the best food. The dishes for the wedding party included sour-cooked pork, boiled dumplings, cabbage with peas, buckwheat, bread and a very deep pie.

Later the women would often moan about the wedding house. They might tell tales about how the hosts let their own people into the room before the feast, to gobble all the best titbits: 'I seen with my own eyes, out they come, fat dripping down their chins. While they was dancing around I had to go home to find something to eat, that's why I only put half a rouble in for the bonnet.' Or, 'You must have seen it, the candle on the altar was flickering, the whole time! Oy, that man's going to beat her. And she could've turned him down, she's still young, some bachelor could've had her, don't she know how he battered his dead wife?' etc.

In the country All Saints' Day is also observed with great reverence. As early as two weeks before All Saints' Day, people give money for what they call *wypominki*. These are prayers for the Souls of the Deceased. For several weeks, the priest and others pray for these Souls after the sermon. The priest takes some money for every Soul. People dressed the graves with all kinds of twigs, sprinkled sand over them, or made wreaths from tissue paper – red and other bright colours.

Then when the day came there was an evening procession, and after they returned nobody went outside. Not even to their next-door neighbours or into their own yard. They used to say, 'All Saints' Day belongs to the dead folk so we mustn't disturb them.' Once I asked why. A woman we knew explained that the Souls will appear to nosey people. She told me how a certain peasant thought he was clever and went out to the mill that night, 'And when he got there all of a sudden the wind blows and howls, so miserably this bloke feels the shivers running up and down his spine from the terror. He looks, and all his grain is in the dirt under his cart, there's no holes in the sacks, they're all tied up, but there's nothing left inside 'em. Terror seizes him, he wants to fly, but the horses stand like stones and won't budge, so he has to run away all by himself. This is a warning, you see, you must spend that night praying for the Souls – not meddling with 'em.' I said to the woman, 'Perhaps the Souls don't haunt us at all, but people are scared because of the stories,' but the woman replied, 'Miss, it's all true whatever you think. There was another man ventured out on All Souls' Night, and all of a sudden his horses froze. Stuck there. They feel heavy, they can't move. He has a good look, feels about in the dark – and he finds something lying in the cart, some thing, hairy and huge. He was in such a fright, covered in sweat, he couldn't hardly reach home. After that he got sick. It seems he never spoke a word for two days except when they asked him, what's happened to the horses? He tells 'em, "I don't know, it could be some Souls who was out walking for a penance got tired and took 'em. Never mind though," says the peasant, "Shame about the horses, but let it be a warning to you all: don't mess with spirits." After that he spent his whole life only praying, he wouldn't go out, and I still feel the shivers going up and down my spine as I think of it.'

On another occasion a peasant told me that everything people say about the Souls is true. 'Because one big-head said he'd only believe things if he saw 'em with his own eyes. So he took a ladder, put it up against the church window, and he tries to peek in – because they said the last parish priest, who was dead, used to come back to celebrate the Mass with all the parish Souls, like a shepherd with his sheep. Now, whenever this peasant steps on a rung of the ladder, it snaps. But somehow he got up to the window. And when he peered in and saw what was going on – all the Souls are kneeling, and there's the priest celebrating just like he was alive – he went numb from fear.'

Anyway, the common people were terribly superstitious when I was young. They used to say, if a mother dies leaving orphans behind, she always comes back after death and breastfeeds the youngest in the night. I say, 'But surely the dead don't have breast milk,' but as a woman explained to me, an old granny saw it with her own eyes because her daughter used to come back at night, kneel beside the cradle, and feed her baby. And the granny claimed there was just a sort of swoosh when she went back to Heaven, the door didn't even open. I loved listening to the people in the village telling me tales about the ghosts and other times. It never crossed my mind that one day I would be talking to you about the dreadful ignorance people lived in.

The priest lived in the manor house with the gentry while the common people were left totally to themselves. They had a strong faith in magic. They explained that if a master shepherd wants to, he can 'do it' to anyone. 'Do it' means 'put you under a spell'. Evidently this happened in Radoszewice. The squire dismissed his master shepherd, and he put a spell on him in revenge. 'The spell was such that he couldn't pass a stool, except inside his trousers. So this squire couldn't ever go out amongst people, couldn't go nowhere, 'cos whenever he tried he straight away soiled his underwear and had to stay home. They say his butlers didn't like working for him.' Such was the power of the master shepherd. 'More 'n once, if a neighbour had a grudge against another neighbour he'd go to the master shepherd and pay him to cast a spell. He could send lumbago, or a fever as won't go away.' A master shepherd apparently drew his power from the fact that at some point during the full moon he would dig up a dead Jew from the Jewish cemetery and bury him in the sheepfold under the threshold. A sacked shepherd could also make the sheep disobey the new man. 'They'd flock up close together and, do what you will, they would not move or a disease'd strike 'em all dead.'

The women believed in black magic. If a woman came for milk after sunset, she never got it or if she did you had to sprinkle salt, because otherwise your cow would go dry. If two neighbours had an argument, they instantly started shouting at each other 'you witch': 'You come to get milk after sunset, don't you? You bitch, d'you think people don't know your mother was a witch too? You think no one saw her churning butter at night, stark naked?' Or sometimes there were women who, if they merely looked at something, then – *zmykało*. I think *zmykało* meant it was instantly ruined.

People also believed in exorcism. Apparently the priest in Brzyków had the power to expel the Devil. An old woman told me she was just back from his church, where he had been casting the Devil out. 'They brought this possessed woman to the church, but soon as the Devil saw they was going to drive him out, he wouldn't let her near it. He roared, he threw himself around inside the woman, there's foam spewing from her gob. Then the priest blessed her 'n prayed for her 'n the Devil started doing terrible things – but the priest he just carried on blessing. The woman starts to howl. And suddenly there's fire in her mouth, and smoke, and that's when the Devil left.' People also believed that 'If a howling dog looks upwards, then it's certain there'll be a fire. If on the other hand he howls head down, death's coming. There's always omens before anyone dies. Either a picture will have fallen off the wall, or there'll be such a frightful bang as us all shivers, or there'll be some sort of spook.'

People in the village used witchcraft to treat various ailments. They had faith in healers. A healer usually treated people with incense. He ignited herbs on a lid and circled the sick person several times, saying prayers and burning the incense. It was supposed to be the best remedy for most illnesses. If someone had a swollen face or boils, though, the healer used other cures. He recommended passing stools onto a dirty rag. That was to disgust the illness and frighten the pain away. More often than not, it seems to me, it was the patient who went away after that treatment, to Heaven. If somebody had a headache, people had to lift the spell. Exceptionally, someone went to Osjaków and fetched a medic. The medic treated every condition. He even used cupping if someone had a bad stomach, and as for teeth, he extracted them using small pliers or he applied root treatment by numbing the teeth with *krauzet* or alum. Of course that was a temporary measure, the teeth rotted afterwards.

I remember that things improved, medically speaking, in Osjaków later on. This was when Father Michnikowski came to the parish; he was quite good at administering treatments. If you wanted to reach the nearest doctor you had to transport the patient, who was often gravely ill, twenty kilometres to Wieluń. Usually they died during the journey. People were afraid of doctors. They said, 'No need for a doctor, 'cos "If you're sick to death, don't waste the doctor's breath", better fetch a priest. After a priest, things will turn for the better.' I was a witness when some parents brought their child to the priest for treatment. The child had croup and by the time they made the journey from another parish, the child was dead. Such was medical care.

Pregnant women were dreadfully scared of the midwives. In the country the midwives in the villages usually had no medical knowledge. They often came to a patient straight from the field or some other dirty work with terribly filthy hands and clothes, and so many young women died afterwards from infection or bleeding. The midwife wasn't simply dirty, she was heartless too, insisting you must save the baby before the mother. Because if the baby died unchristened it would suffer eternal damnation, whereas the mother was christened already.

A priest told me he was summoned to a sick woman who would soon be with Lord Jesus. He was horrified by what he saw. The cottage was full of old women, the patient was barely alive, and the village midwife was heating a hooked poker in the fire. The priest asked, 'What are you going to do with that hook?' The midwife said, 'Baby won't come 'cos it's stuck in the girdle. So, Father, I'll catch its ear with this hook and drag it out. Then it won't stay inside mum when she's dead, humph, and we can christen it.' The priest called the man and told him to rush to Wieluń and fetch Doctor Domagalski, who managed to save the woman.

At the second birth I attended – I went with a woman I knew – it transpired that the husband had to fetch a gynaecologist. Of course the old women tried to shout us down, saying that if a doctor comes both the mother and the child are bound to die. But the doctor arrived and gave a general anaesthetic because he had to carry out a difficult procedure. The baby was massive of course and weighed fourteen pounds after they took out its brain, but the mother survived. The doctor told the women the patient must go on a diet, because after a serious operation there was a risk of post-partum fever. My friend was afraid the women would do things their own way the second the doctor left. She proved to be dead right when they tried to feed the patient eggs fried solid. My friend was so alarmed, she tossed the eggs into a bucket of pigswill and took care of the patient by herself until she got better. Those women had strong constitutions. I remember a woman who gave birth while raking oats in the field, walked home by herself (I don't know how she did it, it was quite far away), and a few hours later gave birth to another baby. She even said she felt no need to lie down.

Newborn babies were usually reared with no special care. Not only was hygiene never mentioned, but tiny children had to get along without being looked after. People usually bathed babies in the same bowls where they kneaded dumplings and bread. The baby had very little clothing. Nappies were made from some ghastly scraps of rag. A tiny baby would be taken to the fields. They used to arrange three sticks there, so that sheets could be tied to them to create a kind of hammock, which the mothers put pillows in. You couldn't see the baby in this cradle. They were always sweating and overtired from being rocked, because another little child kept rocking the cradle.

The older children were unsupervised too. I did see mothers finding some time, usually on Sunday, to wash a child and clear off the insects. Village women, even the richer ones, were always overworked. They had to labour in the fields, tend the poultry, pigs and cows. Usually women worked in both field and farmyard, and so their children and their dwellings were in a miserable state. There was a lot of work even in winter – wool had to be carded by hand. They used special brushes with wire bristles. Then there was wool to be spun, linen. Plucking feathers was better, because girls from several homes would get together after supper for an evening and all work together. Of course that was more cheerful, together you could sing, joke, gossip. The hostess would always prepare some nice food. After the plucking, there was coffee and white bread and dancing.

Things were always tidier in winter, because daughters – usually unmarried women – came home from Germany. They brought their mothers all kinds of German clothes, pots, bowls. It was when people began going to Germany that they started getting enamelware, better clothes. Because people in the villages usually wore homespun garments – long russet coats for the men, or black or dark blue. A russet coat was decorated with shiny buttons, trousers were tucked in the boots. Women wore bright woollen clothes and woollen aprons. Even their jackets were homespun. Round the neck they wore ruffs and layers of necklaces. Sometimes they used their aprons as headscarves. Children were poorly dressed. Boys up to the age of twelve and fifteen wore trousers sewn up to a bodice with sleeves; it looked very unattractive.

There were lots of paintings in their homes. There were tiny pictures under big pictures, as well as little pictures in-between big pictures. The walls were literally covered with devotional objects and coloured paper cut-outs. The table too was dressed with holy figurines and a cross. And there were bouquets of tissue paper flowers. In my days people didn't usually have chairs, there were benches. They used wooden ladles to draw water. Beds were covered with a high pile of bedding. Sometimes the pillows reached the ceiling. They stacked them on one side of the bed.

There was usually no flooring. After sweeping the ground, women sprinkled sand over it. They swept up a lot of dust. In the dwellings there were lots of flies. I was most cross when I saw how unhygienic the bread-baking was. Women would put loaves under their bedclothes so the dough would rise in the warmth. House-proud women put a clean sheet under the bread, but most just stuck the bread in bed in the morning, after chasing the children out of it. Cottages were whitewashed with lime. The ceiling wasn't whitewashed for a few years after they built it, but scrubbed with a wet broom. Outside, the cottage was whitewashed often. There were plenty of flowers in the windows, usually geraniums, but they didn't look very nice there because people grew them in cracked pots. When the girls came back from Germany, homes were much tidier. They also learned knitting in Germany and made the family stockings and mittens.

I was very young when I lived in the village, so it's difficult for me to describe the peasant's attitude to the manor, or the peasant's psychology in general. He was distrustful, because the manor never lifted a finger to get closer to the village. The peasant disliked the manor because he had to work on the lord's estate for fifteen kopecks a day under the harsh hand of a steward. They said that when Adam Krasowski went to a ball, he wiped his bottom with thirty-five-rouble notes. The servants knew him well. They looked forward to it.

There was too little space in the village to build houses at a proper distance. They built them right beside each other or just a few metres apart. People stored firewood, branches, chopping-blocks and so forth in the gaps. One day a fire broke out. It was just before the harvest, people were in the church. The fire started in a cottage and they say the whole village went up in smoke. There were no fire brigades in the countryside. People had hand pumps which were useless, the fire spread so quickly. Over ninety houses burnt down in two hours. A great deal of livestock burnt – mainly pigs and horses because the cows were grazing in the fields. It was a hideous sight. Even things people managed to rescue from their homes were burnt in the fields. Some children and women burnt to death in the fire. There were no fire hoses to put it out, because peasants were taught to have poles ready with rags attached and to smother a fire with that. Some people ran round the flames holding pictures of St Agatha and poured St Agatha's salt into the fire to drive it from their homes.

The manor could make an agreement with a peasant for the land to be parcelled out. Most peasants said: 'We'd have to pay the bank, and the lord of the manor will grab the land back whenever he chooses, he'll always dig up some law or other.'

They thought they were being astute. There were a handful of wise peasants, though, especially one named Dobras. My father took him and another poor farmer, Rabokowski, to see the Governor-General's wife who lived in Odessa and they bought a few hundred acres of land from her. They paid for it through a bank. Other small farmers saw that those who took the risk were doing better, but they scratched their heads and still they said, 'They'll never make it, either the leaseholder or the government'll take it back.' They were so terribly distrustful. But Wojciech Dobras twirled his moustache, smiled wisely and a touch mockingly, and said: 'Neighbours, you can worry about it till they've took the lot away from me. Worry and eat dry bread. But me, while I wait, I'll spread my bread with butter 'n honey. Let's see who ends up best off.' Well, the land never was taken away. The next generation is farming it today.

Wojciech Dobras was enlightened although he couldn't write. He always wished there had been a school there. Since there wasn't, he asked my father to teach his children to read and write. The children were clever of course, and even though my father only spent an hour a day teaching them, they learned to read and write quickly. Meanwhile Dobras twirled his moustache, happy that his children would know more than the neighbours' children. Besides, he had a great deal of common sense. He had Jewish lodgers, so when Father Chrzanowski made house calls on his parishioners, he refused to pay a pastoral visit to Dobras' house because of those 'lice-ridden sheep'. Dobras' wife cried quietly, his children were sad because they got no holy pictures from the priest, but Dobras simply said, 'Wait till I drop a rouble in his collection plate, he won't bother to ask did this rouble come from a Jew's rent, he'll snap it up. And if they have a baby, I'll take it to the Governor-General himself to order the christening. I won't listen to nobody, there wouldn't be Jews in the world unless Jesus wanted.' Dobras was very fond of horses. They were his great love. Honestly, no one else in Szynkielew had such beautiful horses. One day thieves stole a pair from him. With all his peasant stubbornness he spent six months going round the markets, until he recognised them somewhere near Kraków and after a few court cases got them back. Even a dog in Dobras' house looked better than other dogs. The man wasn't a patriot; he didn't know about Polish history. He often told me how his father fought against his lord in the Parzymiechy uprising, where the gentry were defeated and sang: *It's a sin, it's a sin, Parzymiechy done us in!* His audience was very amused by that.

The peasants were very accepting of the times they lived in. I never heard anyone complaining that Poland was in bondage. They used to say about the Tsar: 'Our lord and master knocks spots off Mr Wilhelm.' Some had a portrait of the Tsar's family nailed up among the other pictures. But equally, those who travelled to Germany brought back portraits of Mr Wilhelm and his family, and put them up.

I often chatted with people on Sundays, when they came to have their correspondence with relatives in Germany written or read out to them. I tried to tell them that if we were not in bondage, we'd be much better off. Because as things are, who cares about the Poles? 'Let them suffer in poverty!' I could see they were not convinced, they quickly changed the subject. These were the things they liked to talk about amongst themselves: 'Why's the Tsar taking so long to give us the gentry's land?' 'Maybe we'd be better off doin' a deal with the manor, the ones who got the land from the Governor's wife are doin' all right.' Some took one view, others took another: 'Don't envy 'em. When it comes to it, they won't even keep their shirts.' And so they went on, smoking their *siekanka,* which was their name for the cheapest tobacco. On nights like that you could hear a lot about someone's twenty-five-year-long service in the Russian army. I'd see old soldiers still wearing the greatcoats in which they returned from the service. Everyone listened to the old soldiers. They had seen the bigger world and its customs. They went to it young, and they came back old. Many forgot their mother tongue or married Russian women.

Very often on summer nights they took their animals to eat clover in the squire's field. Usually they went with their horses. Many a horse gorged itself and burst. At night the farmers watched their own flocks. They would tell stories about ghosts and plagues and wars. Everything they said, they knew from hearsay, because of course they couldn't read. Everything was passed along, mouth to mouth.

I also remember 'the Barracks'... That was the nickname for the poor homes on the manor farm. The roofs were full of holes, you could slide on the clay floors after it rained. Around the Barracks were cesspits. The children went dirty and hungry because their mothers had to labour on the estate. Sometimes I walked with my Mummy through the village and she would say, 'The masters ride in their carriages and give fine balls, they'd do better to found an orphanage for these children.' And I'm thinking, 'Perhaps it isn't as bad as Mummy says. When the mistress or the master walk through the village, I see old people and even children kiss their hands.' I ask Mummy, 'Why do they kiss them, if they are so bad?' Mummy says to me, 'They have to, because they're poor.'

Stefania Różewicz

9 october, 1921

Stefania Różewicz

I HADN'T BEEN FEELING very well all day. In the evening I went out to say the Rosary and on the way back from church I started feeling pains that kept me from returning home. And then I became afraid I might give birth to my child in the street. I was leaning against a wall when I was approached by a lady I knew who helped me home. Two hours later at nine I had a son.

I was slightly disappointed because I had really been wishing for a daughter. He was a healthy plump baby. He had little black curls reaching nearly halfway down his neck. The baby was exceptionally quiet. His father was proud he had another son. His older brother Januszek kept on asking, how did the stork bring his little brother. His father had to open the casement window and showed him how the stork noticed that one window wasn't quite shut and so dropped his little brother off.

Our newborn son was so calm, slept beautifully. Sometimes I got up at night just to look in his cot and check that he hadn't smothered himself by any chance, he was so quiet. At his christening we gave him the name Tadeusz, because this was what his big brother really wanted. I asked him, 'Januszek, what name shall we give your brother?' He replied 'Tadeusz Kościuszko.' He took a liking to it because we had a big portrait of General Kościuszko hanging on the wall.

The christening took place several weeks after my son was born. For godparents, we asked some people we knew: we asked a colleague from the court to be godfather, the godmother was a neighbour. The godparents dressed up for the occasion. My baby boy wore white for his christening, as was the fashion of the time: silk and lace. We had quite a few guests at the christening. Everyone was amazed by the baby. We drove to church in a *droshky*. We went with our servant girl and our elder son, who kept asking if we took him to be christened like this too when he was a baby.

At home after the christening the godparents gave me back the baby, with best wishes for both baby and me. To commemorate the occasion the godparents left their godson a little money on his pillow. Well, later on after the christening there was drink, food and endless talk about the hero of the day: the fact that he never cried during the christening like other babies, the fact that he didn't even pull a face when the priest put salt in his mouth. Some said, 'Look how plump and pink he is, perhaps he'll be a priest, he should be called Franek.' The guests ate and drank and raised toasts, because there was no shortage of drink. Fathers always took care of that. Father said, '"A guest in the house is God in the house", and since it's a son, we have to drink double to show respect. A daughter is a child too,' said Father, 'but she doesn't count as much as a boy.' So they ate and drank and sang some sentimental songs, some patriotic ones, ended with 'Let him live a hundred years...', 'Let's love each other', and they all went home. My servant girl was pleased, because the guests were in a good mood and liked the whole household so, as they say, they didn't stint on the tips.

In 1921 when our son Tadeusz was born we lived in Reymont Street. We had two small rooms with a kitchen and a hall. It was just after the war, it was almost impossible to find anywhere to live. You needed a police escort to move in. And we had to put up Father's colleague with his wife and little girl. We had to cope with that for about two years. I often escaped with our children to the countryside.

We were so poor it was very hard to get food. I remember Father used to bring rations of brown beans and barley from his office. The bread was awful, I think it was rationed. Some said the bread was made from lupins: as I remember it was like a mix of chaff and bran. Our diet was wretched, mostly potato dumplings, cabbage, beans and *krupnik* barley soup. Lard was very hard to get hold of. The butchers got rich quick. You often had to walk two or three kilometres to buy a bit of lard under the counter. People ate meat twice a week at the most.

Winter 1921 was severe, there was a great frost; we burnt peat for fuel because coal was scarce. I don't remember the prices of food and clothes exactly. Everything must have been expensive because when Father took a loan worth a month's salary, it was just enough to buy some poor quality cloth to make trousers. A month's salary wasn't enough to pay a tailor as well. The money coming in couldn't buy us clothes. Usually everything was purchased with an IOU, which you often had to get extended in someone's office. Clerks and teachers, they generally bought things on instalments or with an IOU. There were a lot of clerks around then, and they could borrow money at interest: ten *złotych* a month per hundred. If such a clerk couldn't pay it all off quickly, he would just pay the interest. Ten months later he would have paid 100 *zł*, and what he owed on the IOU was still the same.

Immediately after the war, children got extra nutrition from American aid. This American food consisted of rice pudding, beans, cocoa, wheat rolls. As for clothes, there were some second-hand things, mostly shoes. Charities gave them out. Father had no winter coat that year, he turned a blanket into a coat, and I bought some shoes on instalments. You couldn't buy anything at Generowicz's. When I was expecting my baby I couldn't get a pallet, so I made one out of cotton curtains with a flower design. And my son was born in a flowerbed.

I remember everything went up day by day. By 1924 we were counting in millions. They changed the money in 1924. After that the prices of food and clothing started falling. From about 1926, if I remember correctly, people started dressing up, buying furniture, and eating better.

My parents are getting ready to go visiting;
before I was born

But going back to my little boy born on 9th October 1921; the baby was healthy and developing nicely, his first tooth came at six months. This caused great joy at home. Our servant girl spotted the tooth and got a present for it. I breastfed the baby for nine months. In his eighth month, in May, I had him inoculated against smallpox. A doctor from Wieluń inoculated him in Osjaków. I was very happy that day, because the doctor lifted my son up high over his head and said, 'See, mothers, every child should look so clean and healthy.' In June the baby caught dysentery and was seriously ill for a good month, barely conscious from the weakness, but in the first days of July he started picking up and smiled at a white horse.

Baby's first word was 'mama'. When he was only one, the child could say a number of words clearly: he called the servant girl 'Aśka' because he heard us saying 'Staśka', and he called his older brother 'Usek' because of 'Januszek'. Baby started walking by himself when he was a year and a month: he was desperate to run by then but couldn't yet do it. I used to take a towel and hold it round his waist and support him that way.

The kiddie always amused us with his various reactions and sayings which only he could understand, inside his own world of sights and thoughts. If he was in a field trying to pick an ear of wheat or rye and couldn't do it, he would shout at it: 'Let go, let go.' He must have thought someone was holding it under the ground. And when he took offence at something, he used to disappear under the table calling, 'I've gone away into the world.' When he wasn't two yet, I had an illness in my kidneys. I remember he came to my bed crying and said, 'Mummy, let it hurt you, but don't die.' He was generally very interested in everything, in animals most of all.

In his third year the child could already say a short prayer by heart. He had a good heart, the little one, was very compassionate. He was so tiny, and yet if he saw a poor old man or woman he would run after them and say, 'Come to us and Mummy will give you something.' I remember a conversation I had with my husband once. I was supporting a cousin studying at the *gymnasium,* who always said he wanted to be a priest. Things were becoming hard for us. I told my husband, 'My cousin needs to make it on his own, perhaps he should go and live in lodgings.' It never occurred to me that the child could even hear what we were saying, but Tadzio comes up and says, 'Mummy, do you want to go to Hell or Heaven?' I say, 'Well, darling I'd like to be in Heaven.' The kiddie says, 'But you'll be in Hell.' I ask, 'But why?' And he says, 'He wants to be a priest and you say he must go away.' That argument sank into me deeply.

His elder brother was already six by then, Tadzio was three years younger. They played together very well. The kiddie's questions and curiosity quite often amazed me. 'But why,' he always asked, 'but what, but when?' On one occasion he asked a neighbour a question. She told him she is poor now, but used to have a mill and lots of turkeys and ducks. And the child says: 'But Miss, you should have saved the ducks and turkeys in your tummy, to take out now one by one, and then you wouldn't be hungry.' My older boy Januszek always said, 'I want to write stories,' because he loved listening and reading (at the age of five), whereas Tadzio said when he was three: 'I want to do carving or be a farmer, I'll have a horsey and a cottage and a field.'

In 1924 I had my third son. And just as Father showed Januszek where the stork dropped off his little brother when Tadzio was born in 1921, now I showed Tadzio how his new brother Staś was dropped into the attic through the smoke hole.

Tadeusz was born on 9th October 1921 in Radomsko, in 12 Reymont Street, near the little river Radomka.

Stefania Różewicz

hands shackled

The bars split the light
that floods onto blinded eyes
onto hopeless hours
on the hopeless night

An open mouth like a wound
and the hands the shackled hands
and the wracked bodies
where the mothers stand

The mothers' fragile hands
twisted by horror and blood
make the word flesh
make the light God

Crying our sons like yours
were defenceless and small
for their sake and for your small son
take the pain from them all

Let one star slip through the bars
give the blinded eyes light
shine on the hopeless hours
shine on the hopeless night.

twice condemned

I see a smile
pulled down from the white face
against the wall.

Death's messenger a Stranger
bent his head
lower.

I see
a comic statue of anguish
in flapping slippers
by the stove
a small crooked
figurine
of a petrified mother.

dead fruit

Here are the golden pears on the plate
the flowers and the two young girls

On the table the photo of a youth
upright and bright in the black kepi

The girls have such soft lips
the girls have such sweet eyes

The poor mother steps across the room
adjusts the photograph and cries

The gold suns on the table darken
as does the dead fruit of her life.

chestnut

It's saddest of all to leave
home on an autumn morning
when there's no promise of a prompt return

The chestnut in front of the house
planted by father grows before our eyes

mother is little
and you can carry her in your arms

on the shelves stand jars
in which jams
like sweet-lipped goddesses
preserve the taste
of eternal youth

the army in the back of the drawer
will remain lead till the world ends

and the omnipotent God who stirred
gall into sweetness
hangs on the wall helpless
and badly painted

Childhood is like the blurred face
on a gold coin that rings
clear.

the wall

She's turned her face to the wall

oh but she loves me
why has she turned away from me

and so with one twist of the head
you can turn your eyes
from a world where sparrows tweet
and young people stroll about
showing off loud ties

She's alone now
facing the dead wall
and will stay so

she'll stay up against the wall
as it swells
she small and twisted
with her fist clenched

while I sit
with legs of stone
and don't snatch her up from that place
do not lift her
lighter than a sigh.

return

Suddenly the window will open
and mother will call me
time to go in

the wall will split
I'll enter heaven in muddy boots

I'll sit at the table and spit
answers to questions

there's nothing wrong with me
leave me alone. With my head in my hands
I sit and sit. How can I
tell them about this long
and tangled road.

Here in heaven mothers are knitting
green woollen scarves

flies buzz

father is napping by the stove
after six days' labour.

No – but I can't can I
tell them about men
tearing each other's throats.

burial mound

They've raised a burial mound over him
made of arrivals and departures
of time and space
of people things events
butter coffee newspapers
of albums bound in green velvet
flowers bromide
and artificial laughter

Almost everybody's come
on the table lies a copper leaf
here they drop the ash

Mother digs in the mound
and excavates a young head
in a ray of light
with its tobacco-scented
wide mouth

it's him
the one you don't rush to welcome
at the front door
the one who isn't dozing in the raspberry bushes
the one who won't come back tomorrow

Mother buried alive
at the table
limply moves her fingers
in the air.

playing horsey

A canary
yellow as a lemon
in a wire basket

granny in a bonnet
caught
in a net of wrinkles

father with his forehead hidden
in a cloud of smoke

the boys neighing
manes flowing with the wind
knock their hooves
into the impatient earth

mother has caught
a magnificent steed
in white braces
and kisses his sour muzzle
full of sorrel

but whoever sees...

But whoever sees my mother
in a steel blue robe in a white hospital
shivering
suffering
with a wooden smile
with white gums

She who had faith for fifty years
but now cries and says
'I don't know... don't know'

her face is like a huge cloudy tear
she puts her yellow hands together like
a scared little girl
and her lips are navy blue

but whoever sees my mother
a frightened small animal
with a bulging eye

he –

I'd like to carry her on my heart
and feed her sweetness.

a woman in black walks on roses

She turns her yellow face gnawed
by worries towards the good
sun and then the smile
now only a half-healed wound
lights her up.

On the path of her waning life
she sees one rose
so she too had her bed of roses
stooping over this
strange flower from the world
of the living she thinks about crushed
happiness.

She thinks of the sons who left
her in rough uniforms
they went off stamping and other women
threw red roses
under their iron feet.

And the youngest born with
a silver spoon marched off in a steel
helmet and she couldn't
stroke his head
then she ran after them wracked by
the flame of the great gold trumpets.

Now she walks this path
alone and carries a small loaf
she needn't share anymore.

She turns her gutted face towards the sun.

Here blemished light
falls on a stone path
on a path of iron crosses
on a path of black marble
from which emerge statuettes
of white plump children.

A sweet bunch of dead cherubs
hangs from the sky.

wicked son

I look through the window
with its pink flower frame

outside cats are getting drenched
and my old mother
draws some murky water
with saintly hands

in the window with a sly smile
her son stands

1941

the tear

To Mother

Day after day topples
and the memory recedes

Of the years that passed
like a passing sigh

Although blood and terror
burst out of them

But just sometimes
shadows reappear

And are passed from the eyes to the breast
in a stream of tears

Washing away faults
that are merely human

And again we run
to the light's domain

There is a day a Day coming
like a bird in flight

The day has swallowed darkness
and it shines starlight

1951

In April 1944 I came home from 'the woods' on a pass from my partisan unit. It made Mum happy...

return to the woods

When I close my eyes I sense
A bird's call the creak of pines
The wood's shallow silence
Ruffled by our laughter

I see the wood where
We picked berries together
Our bodies then were as bubbling
And young as the waters

We rushed back home
Bare feet like wings fly
And shine in the dust
Our mouths black from berries

Now you can see the house Smoke
In the sky creeping patiently
And mother in the window
Her hand shielding her eyes

a small house

I – a small house for the dead
here they found their
last shelter

hands gesturing
in my direction
take me
take me with you
don't let go

I was opened
and they moved in
to the cold
the void
the dark

this is
their
eternal light
sin's absolution
the body's resurrection

this is the everlasting life

❋ ❋ ❋

Assisi a nest
on a cracked rock
a bird's white
egg

I carried
this rosying
landscape
towards my city

I never succeeded

on the third day
your smile
deteriorated
I returned You to the earth

here flows the river
of forgetting
over the eyes the mouth
over your feet
shod in paper
slippers

* * *

At dawn the light
draws mother's
ashen face
in charcoal

Lights the stove
makes the hearth and home

the kindling crackles
the scent of sap in the wood
the flame spreads
and roars

in the window I see the sky
in the sky the sun
your faces stand around
their lines
will not be drawn again

1963

door

In a dark room
on a table there's
a glass of red wine

through an open door
I see the landscape of childhood
a kitchen with a blue kettle
the heart of Jesus in a crown of thorns
mother's translucent shadow

in the round silence
a cock crows

the first sin
a white seed in a green
fruit soft
slightly bitter

the first pink devil
moving the hemispheres
beneath a silk polka dot
dress

opening slightly
in the illuminated landscape
the third door
and through it in the mist
in the distance
a bit to the left
or at the centre

I see
Nothing

1966

thorn

I don't believe
I don't believe from waking
to sleeping

I don't believe from the edge to the edge
of my life
I don't believe just as openly
deeply
as my mother
deeply believed

I don't believe while
eating the bread
drinking the water
loving the body

I don't believe
in his priests his symbols
inside his temples

I don't believe in a city street
in the fields in the rain
the air
inside the golden annunciation

I read his parables
straight as a stem of wheat
and I think of a god
who never laughed

I think of a little
god bleeding
in the white
swaddling bands of childhood

about the thorn that rips open
our eyes mouth
now
and in the hour of death

golden mountains

The first time
I saw mountains
I was
twenty-six

I didn't laugh
didn't shout
face to face with them
I whispered

When I got back home
I wanted to tell
mother
what mountains look like

It was hard to convey
at night
everything looks different
both mountains and words

Mother was silent
maybe she fell asleep
tired

In the clouds
the moon grew larger
the golden mountain
of the poor

1955

* * *

I shouted at Her
ten years ago

she departed
in slippers made of black
shiny paper

'don't try to explain'
she said
'no need'

I shouted at Her
in an empty
hospital corridor

it was july the heatwave
oil paint peeling
off the walls

the scent of linden trees
in a city park covered
in soot

I godless
wanted to cry her a meadow
when as she was dying
gasping she pushed back at
the empty and frightening beyond

for a blink of an eye she returned
to herself and her village
in the last hour
I wanted to beg for her
a tree
a cloud a bird

I see her feet tiny
in large paper
coffin slippers

sitting between
the table and the coffin
godless I wished for a miracle
in a gasping industrial city
in the second half
of the 20th century

this thing's crying
dragged from me
into the light

* * *

I was beating my way through the dream
heavily
before waking
in warm streams of
tears words
mother was coming towards me
Don't be afraid you're in the earth I kept saying
no-one can harm you any more nor hurt nor touch you
seized by that fear mother
hugged me
don't be afraid you're in the earth
you are inside me no one will touch you
nor humiliate nor hurt you
I was beating my way through that dream heavily
in front of me stood a Shadow

A postcard of mysterious Erbalunga,
a small place at the northern end of Corsica

the photograph

today I received
an old postcard from a foreign country
a picture of Erbalunga

I've never heard the name
and I don't know where it is
and I don't want to

Erbalunga

yesterday I received
a salvaged photograph of mother
from 1944

mother in the photograph
is still young beautiful
smiles slightly

but on the back
I read written
in her hand the words
'year 1944 cruel to me'

in the year 1944
the Gestapo murdered
my older brother

we concealed his death
from mother

but she saw through us
and concealed it
from us

red stamps

THE BAILIFF'S COME. Huge, dark. Except for a few threads of silver glimmering in his beard. He grunted something, made a note in his rustling papers. He walked around our flat examining the furniture. Huger and huger he grew, darker and darker. His assistant, a plump painted woman, smiled. Every piece of furniture they touched began to die. The warmth vanished. We looked on, frightened, wondering would the bailiff stick one of those stamps of his onto our good old cupboard. Would he pull out our soldiers from the two drawers, and the little animals safe in matchboxes.

We whispered. The furniture stood against the walls like coffins now. The flat grew cold.

It was not until my brother and I crept into the creaking bed and hid our heads under the thick eiderdown that we dared speak out loud. We prayed for a miracle.

But in the cold light of the morning, five red stamps bled like five wounds.

a memory from 1929

IT WAS THE GREAT WINTER. Apple and pear trees split and
cracked, struck by the frost's white axe. Sparrows collapsed into
our kitchen or lay dead on the earth. Mother sent me round to
our unemployed neighbours with a mug of hot borscht.

The head of the family lay under a thick red eiderdown to
which his white goatee had frozen. He saw the steaming mug
and tugged at his goatee to try to get it free. The eiderdown
made an ominous sound. I was frightened the old man's goatee
would snap, so I began to breathe on it. The goatee thawed. The
old man ate the borscht and dumplings and wiped his mouth.
He put on his glasses and reached for a book with a bright
cover. Letter by letter I deciphered the title: Henry Ford, *My
Philosophy of Industry.*

The old man gave me a knowing wink, wrapped himself in
the red eiderdown, and began to read.

Mum in her formal outfit

Father in his formal outfit.
That was how people used to pose for photographs

father

Strolling through my heart goes
my old father
Never saved in his life
never hoarded
grain upon grain
never bought himself a little cottage
or a gold watch
somehow it never added up

Lived like a bird
liltingly
from day to day
but
tell us how can
a junior clerk live like this
for years

Strolling through my heart goes
father
in an old hat
whistling
a jolly tune
And believing sure as hell
he's bound for heaven

1954

granddad's visit

To the Good Old Man

Father paid us a visit
'Wife' I say 'bring out the glasses
The old man's frozen to the bone
Make his bones feel
at home!'

Granddad rubs his hands
mumbles something about the weather
'no need I'm not
hungry darling'
he tiptoes to the cot
full of pillows peeps
spots his grandson asleep
knock knock knock surprised
Janek opens his grey little eyes
squeaks something possibly hello

The vodka makes the table glow
'aqua vitae' granddad cries
and sits at the table
one two three shots
a little warmth spreads
a little ice melts
'third time lucky as the saying goes'
says granddad
'every horse needs four legs'
and then
'four walls and the roof makes five'

after the fifth toast
granddad starts singing a song
'there was a host
who had no house...'
and remembers being young
the family their village
various countries
the fact that he went to St Petersburg
that he lived in a yurt in Siberia
that he drank camel's milk in Kirghizia
and always wanted to play the organ in church
about ghosts maidens married women
and priests' housekeepers
plump white as pigeons
who soon loved more than religion

Granddad bears the cross of his seven decades
never mind bears – he twirls
his cross like a cane
and says
'somehow slowly you do push
the wheelbarrow of life'

Then he knocks on the cot again
picks up his grandson
mumbles something
coochy-coos something
kisses his grey little eyes
shows him chimney smoke in the sky
through the window

Then he gets ready to go
we all give granddad a kiss
and tell him come back for Christmas
The Wife says
'Baby Jaś say something for granddad
tell him that first word you said'
Jaś swaddled in pillows
nods his little head...

1954

the boat

Don't cry
after all you didn't love him
he's an object
to carry out of the house

windows half open discreetly

in my black suit
in a boat
without oars
leaving the world
sailing away
father

a wooden coffin
run aground tangled in flowers
green spruce wreaths
paper ribbons

father lived for
ninety years
died February 1977

don't cry

oh but I did love him
inside my eyelids a tiny image
father carrying an evergreen tree
a stand and an axe
wades

through deep snow
on the table coloured paper chains
stars angel hair

let the earth lie light on him

the two choppers (77)

when Father turned
77
he told me
'the two choppers, Tadziu,
once a man gets
through them, after that
everything gets smooth
as butter'

we got through half a litre of vodka

Father lit up
a leisurely cigarette
and started to blow
smoke rings
ring
by ring

up they floated to the ceiling
spreading out and dispersing

I remember one question
from that birthday conversation of ours
'tell me, Dad,
is life worth living?'

Father studied
the smoke rings

he flicked ash from his cigarette
and said

'course it's worth it!'
then he looked at me
'what's up... Tadziu!...'

Then I understood
that Father loved us
but didn't talk about it

1999

the cobweb shield

[fragment]

[...]

I'M OFF TO THE COUNTRY on a holiday, thirty years ago. The bus leaves from the main square. The little yellow bus. Our 'huge' travel basket is already on the roof. I'm with Mother and my brothers on a leather seat that bounces up and down like a horse. Terror seizes my heart. Isn't that Dubielak up the front, driving today! 'When the Devil's had a drink, he doesn't stop to think.' Everyone knows that, and they're all staring at the back of the driver's battered leather jacket. The engine coughs and snorts. Change the flat tyre.

'Devil Dubielak' took two hours to cover the fifty kilometres. We get out with heads heavy from the fumes. And now we're on a cart, crawling. Wicker baskets are swaying, we're perched on bundles of straw covered with a small kilim rug. In the quiet of the July summer the spokes squeak and grind the sand. Is it the horses or the linden trees that smell of honey? Clear yellow honey. At noon the cart halts in the shade of a tree. We run into the woods. Sun-warmed blackberries in a roadside ditch, covered with white dust, sweeter, smelling of themselves.

The sharp, dry tangle of the woods. A dark blue fog of bilberries. You can get drunk on small fruit. Tiny butterflies, blue and orange.

A huge pine tree creaks.

The spokes sift sand again.

Hours pass. You'll soon see the familiar clearing.

Old Matusek's sitting by the roadside cross with his willow twig.

He's grazing a cow. He used to sit here when my father was a little boy like me. He doesn't hear our voices, doesn't open his eyes. His face is veiled with cobwebs. With rain. With moss. He never went outside the *poviat* of Wieluń.

He never went on the railway.

He used to ask people coming back from Piotrków or Sieradz, 'What's new over the border?'

When he saw his first aeroplane, which looked very like a stork, very like a bat, very like a ladder, he knelt and prayed, 'O Lord in Heaven, take me into your grace.' For the next twenty years he always told people there were two men in the plane. They both had black moustaches, huge glassy eyes, and one played a fiddle. They flew ever so low, brushed the woods with their wings, and then rose to Heaven...

[...]

candlemas

...AT DAWN THAT DAY for as long as I can remember, Mum would set off for Częstochowa. She went there to the Jasna Góra monastery every year. Towards the end of WWI, Father had been struck down by the Spanish Flu sweeping across Europe. The epidemic claimed millions of lives. Father's condition was hopeless and Mother made a vow that for the rest of her life on the 2nd of February, Candlemas, she would go to Częstochowa to the Jasna Góra monastery. I remember the winter of 1929. I was already going to school. The tree trunks were cracking in the orchards and gardens...

Usually Mother would return that evening, but sometimes the train was late and she wouldn't get back until night. For us it was extraordinary, that departure and return... We never went to bed, our vigil was connected to a box of cakes Mum always brought back from Częstochowa. The white box contained ten or twelve cakes and I remember they were cream rolls, little mushrooms with chocolate hats, cream cakes... special cream slices called Napoleons...

gliwice diary

This morning I walked Mother to the hospital.

I can't work.

I can't leave. I have to visit Mother, she's alone there.

But I can't even behave properly – I'm in a rush, I'm empty, she needs affection. Everything grates at home.

I started writing some prose.

It's Saturday – late afternoon. Alone in the empty city. I understand Mother, it's hard for her lying there next to the dying woman.

When she walked away down the corridor she was like a little girl. I love Mother like my own sick little child.

All my poems, I'm convinced, anyway almost all those I'm publishing now, are redundant. They're not created out of necessity.

I begrudge the time spent with my sick mother, I shove the boys out of my study, and then I read old newspapers, pore over the papers with an overstuffed head. I dislike my poems. Can they be beautiful?

Ever since I came back from hospital today, I've felt guilty. I should have stayed longer than the 15 minutes. Then I wanted to go back – it was too late though.

I'm reading *No Dogma* by Sienkiewicz – surely Prus' *Memoirs of a Cyclist* was a deliberate parody. Leon Płoszowski in *No Dogma* is a more serious character, more stupid and funnier. But Prus was wiser than Sienkiewicz. I can't think of any writer today who is Prus' equivalent.

Prus was absolutely contemporary – he lived his times. His *Weekly Chronicles!*

I've been meaning to write an exact record of my last conversation with Staff, and still I haven't done it.

27 MAY 1957, MONDAY

I can't focus. The rage wells up. I'm not resting, not working. I do sit down to write in the morning. There's anxiety in the house – even though it seems calm. Janek was put to bed at one p.m., even though he normally sleeps at three. After scarcely half an hour he's awake and I hear him crying – I go to the bedroom, put his little cardigan on him, give him his books and little gun – ask if he wants to pee. I say Granny Kozłowska's gone to the hospital to visit Granny Różewicz, and he has to stay quiet. For me, of course, it's a waste of time – a break in my lame writing and my total inability to put sentences together. The story is in a pathetic state.

Most poems by contemporary poets (see: *Twórczość,* the French issue) are literary winces. Unless it's broken – smashed... poetry won't ever rise up from its grave.

Drawing from 'the source', folk poetry, is a delusion in our day and age.

1 JUNE 1957

On Friday 31 May at 20:00 I switched on the radio for the evening news. I heard the words: 'Leopold Staff, the doyen of Polish poetry, has died in Skarżysko-Kamienna...' The voice droned on, but I switched off the radio. I went outside.

On Monday 3 June I went to Warsaw for the funeral.

On Tuesday 4 June in the afternoon I went to the Staffs' flat. There was an obituary posted on the wall of the building. It had the name and the surname and the word 'poet' underneath.

Their door was opened by Helena's sister. After two perhaps three hours of conversation I asked her to open the door to the room of My Old Friend. We went in together. I spent about 15 minutes in the room. We talked about Hecunia, the little dog who was put to sleep while the poet was still alive.

12 JUNE 1957

I went to see Mother in hospital.

She kissed my hand and it was... I'd give up my blood to keep her alive.

It was over thirty degrees yesterday, today's hot too. I don't feel like going into the city. I'm feeling alone, discarded by friends. But I'd sooner die alone here than brush up against the Warsaw literati 'moralists'. I keep drifting away even from my closest friends.

And the time, my time: my blood flowing away. A few humorous poems (humour, how?) feeble.

15 JUNE 1957, SATURDAY

Nobody sees how my resources get squandered and shrink in this provincial town, these unending drawn-out years, this isolation and silence. It's June now. Wonderful sunny days – I've been promising myself for years that I'd spend time in the woods, relax... I am stuck in a factory town. Mother is in hospital. 'I don't care anymore', she said yesterday.

Nobody sees me disintegrating, and just as well... My healthy side's yearning for air, water, walks, physical exercise... but I stay here sat between these walls, it's fruitless. A dozen pages scribbled over.

You ought to be writing one single novel or play or one volume of poems all through your life. (Dostoyevsky, Chekhov, Mickiewicz did.)

Writers who write stand-alone stories, novels, poems are superficial. Conrad was writing a poem, one poem, all his life; Żeromski was too. The writers here are busy little bees. They skip from one flower to the next. But it's no good. There's nothing

they can't do and yet it's pointless. I was getting somewhere...
Mind you, Filipowicz, the inner unity seems to be emerging
there, but lately he's distorted it.

What the 'critical' or 'literary' 'fraternity' labelled 'repetition'...
– 'Tadeusz R. keeps repeating himself', they said – was and
possibly still is the most valuable thing in my work. The dogged
reworking, repeating, returning to the same matter, and so on...
to the very end. Other things will get written by somebody else.
There is no alternative. Or you end up with literary chit chat.

17 JUNE 1957, MONDAY

It's hot. Temperatures up to 40 °C. I feel very tired. Can't think.
It's evening, it's difficult to breathe. Can't work. I've been
dreaming for years of spending a month by the sea or in the
woods. I can't make it happen. This year I've even got some
money for it. But I can't go now. And don't want to.

18 JUNE 1957

I am at rock bottom. That's almost funny. There are no rocks
here, it would be hard to explain even to somebody close what
I mean. I am at rock bottom. Used up rhetorical phrase, says
nothing. And still... I know there's no sense or value to what
I'm writing. But I must not scream.

After all there's no point calling for help, I should know that
by now. What illusions have I got left? Who'll hear me? Mother.

Mother is dying day by day. They pump strangers' blood
into her. She's lain there for weeks. She must be afraid of death?
Dr E. keeps praising her as a composed, calm, good patient.
She's not becoming hysterical. But life with a death sentence
(inside you) isn't easy. Particularly when suffering and inactivity
fill the waiting time. I am watching the illness eating Mother.

I touch her little bones wrapped in skin. And feel like...
escaping. But what matters is not what I feel but what I do – I
stay in the city.

I can't organise my life, leisure, not even the work. I don't live like a monk, more like a prisoner without rules. I can't put anything together.

I tend to write very weak stuff now. I wish I could finish this book. I'll earn a break – on parole from writing poems – for a few years. No doubt my muse will show clemency and permit me not to write.

If I worked well this year I could manage:

1/ the book of poems;

2/ the book of short stories;

3/ the play;

4/ the book of Staff's memoirs.

20 JUNE 1957

Corpus Christi.

I'm home. Kamil's at summer camp in Wisła.

Wiesława has been with a friend since Sunday, she went to B. She's preparing for the end of year exams at school. Janek hardly eats and weighs as much as a sparrow.

Zosia R.'s been here, today and yesterday. She visited Mother in hospital. I didn't.

I don't want to accept her illness. I do not want to accept it and I know I am grotesque – I do not want to accept her death. I'm like a mindless animal that won't stop feeding its dead cub. It crams the food into its mouth.

But the doctor said she might still live a few months, she might go to the country.

Note in today's *Trybuna Ludu*: 'Tokyo. Employees of Tokyo's Gunma University announced on Monday that for the first time they have discovered traces of caesium-173, the radioactive isotope which causes harmful hereditary changes, in the Japanese population. Caesium-173, like strontium-90, is dispersed into the atmosphere as a result of nuclear explosions.'

Fragments of a letter from Mother, written before Christmas 1943. At that time I was 'in the woods'

21 JUNE 1957, FRIDAY

Up at 8am. Went to bed late yesterday. A heavy night. Went to Katowice in the morning – for the medication. Though they had it, they wouldn't sell it me. 'You need a prescription' – of course I didn't have one.

I caught the train back to Gliwice. Half the day gone. Then cooked lunch and went to the hospital. From the hospital to Dr Ermich – for the prescription. After I got back from the doctor's – lunch.

I read a newspaper. It's already five. I'm tired, not fit for work. The best hours passed me by.

I don't feel like inventing fiction.

Warsaw (the Literary Union) have sent me a Serbian translation of my story 'The Branch'. Ten Polish periodicals rejected it between 1948 and 1955 – then *Kronika* published it. I looked at the cutting as if it related to some stranger – worse, a stranger long forgotten – and yet it's mine... When my poems go into print now, I look at them like that. Not a grain of joy. Deliberations on God in the Catholic *Tygodnik Powszechny*. Does He exist or not... A letter from a 32-year-old woman: she writes about her life – the Resistance, the Occupation, her husband. Her husband says He doesn't exist, i.e. God. She's not sure etc.

Sometimes I can't go outside until the evening, after dark. When you can't see people's faces – more specifically: the look in their eyes. (Curiously enough such thoughts don't include the pretty faces of girls and young women – is it just an aversion to 'people'...)

Of course at the same time you can love wretched mankind... Anyway, it's all a mystery. How can you loathe the face of a member (even quite clever) of the literati while being delighted by the backside of some young airheaded miss...?

22 JUNE 1957, SATURDAY

12:30. Just back from Katowice – went to the chemist to pick up the medicine. I got up at 6am to catch the 7:30 train – the train was late. The chemist didn't open at 9:00 (as I was informed over the phone by the chemist's assistant), but at 11:00. There was a huge crowd. At two I took dinner and the injections to Mother. At five I went to collect the dishes and took her a tiny bottle of red wine and the Vichy pastilles. Poor sick child. She asked me to pop in tomorrow for a moment, even in the afternoon: 'So I could have a look.' She stroked my hand – 'My lovely son' – I was embarrassed in front of the other sick women lying in the ward. I said, 'Don't talk so loud.' My poor little child.

Janek just came to me – head soaked – he was caught outside in the rain. He asked me to tell him a story. I told him about old Maciej who went to see an elephant at the zoo. Then Janek asked for the little lead elephant on the desk and he went away with it, because I pointed to my notebook and said I'm going to write a book now.

The crowd at the chemist in Katowice didn't just include the needy but black marketeers too.

The chemist's assistant didn't want to talk to me... I begged, 'But please, listen, just listen to me, let me tell you what it is.' Finally she gave in and let me have the medication, the injections. I sit in my 'workshop' and cry. The evenings are worst, and the nights.

I see how she's suffering and I should wish for her release. But I wish so much she could live, so I could scrounge at least half a year more, so I could look at her sometimes. Is this selfishness – but no, love can be like this... she may suffer terribly but let her breathe, let her eyes be open, let her look, let her speak – there's still warmth in this poor, butchered, tormented, human body.

24 JUNE 1957, MONDAY

Yesterday in hospital. Mother on a small chair, in the corridor. Sitting by the window; on the window sill there are two yellow candles stuck in bottles and a bunch of flowers in a jar. Mother's supposed to light the candles when a procession comes down the street (I think it's the Octave of Corpus Christi). Other patients are lined up sitting by other windows. Next to Mother, that 80-year-old woman who eats and sleeps; she's not sick but she's weakening. Mother was given her task by the nun. Mother was nervous there were no instructions how to administer the 'foreign injections' – the doctor on duty didn't know. Mother said she couldn't sleep all night from the worry... 'So expensive.' She was going to insert the glass tube herself to release the gases from her stomach. She's terribly bloated. She was too embarrassed to ask the nurse and ended up with some cuts. Gently stroking her back, I can feel the sharp little bones and I – the healthy one, because 'I'm so tired' – wish I could escape, rest. It's true, even a loving person can be despicable – but no, because I won't escape and leave her alone, surely – it's the thoughts that are despicable – the important thing is what we do. What good would that be, me thinking tender thoughts about the patient while I'm lying on a beach at the seaside. Who cares what thoughts go through my head, if I'm with her, serving – nothing else counts.

I read a story by Kruczkowski in *Trybuna Ludu*: 'Sketches from the Hell of the Righteous'. Reading Camus, *The Fall*. For the last three days I've been going through the typescript of the collected poems coming out next year. Noon. Sweating, angry, without a single thought in my mind, I'm sat at my desk. Doing my unending duty. I sent Father a letter with best wishes and 150 *złotych* for his name day present.

I've not been to see Mother in hospital today. Wiesława took her dinner. Evenings are the worst. Cannot work. Finished correcting the collected poems. I resent the thought of publishing poetry – has the writing become a routine? I dread that.

Mum, I'm wishing you a good night. If only you could sleep, at least. So many sleepless nights.

Alone in the dark. Yesterday you said: 'It's so hard to part from faces, you'd want to look and look.'

My life's come to a halt.

25 JUNE 1957, TUESDAY

I went to see Mother in hospital, I took her some food.

It's 18:00. Just came back home. I was out for a walk. Mother says, 'So they're going,' (she means Janek and Kamil going to the country) and there are tears in her eyes. She's lying down. Her belly swollen with water. Yellow hands, skin and bone. Her head aches, she wrapped it with a towel. Burning oesophagus. Burning liver. What chance do I have with a – malignant tumour?

And the writing... What to do about it?

I'm a lousy writer – a hopeless observer... I don't make any use of my few excursions into 'real life'. When I say 'writer' I mean the prose, poetry's a different story. I can't even wring a few sentences out – and I imagine myself writing books.

Managing time is the main thing. The worst thing. In fact I work from morning to night – haven't taken 'holidays' for years – I should have written three times as much. I don't even play with the boys although I miss it. 'When the pain comes I just curl up and turn to the wall and lie like this quietly...' It isn't just the little bowl of food. She's got to be pulled from the wall, slowly, freed from the bad thoughts. Oh, one is so helpless. I can't accept it, I don't want to give her away.

So they gave the two injections. Without the instructions, 'Why not draw a few syringefuls of water out...' Why these sinful thoughts about going to Kraków.

You're going nowhere now.

28 JUNE 1957, FRIDAY

I came back from Kraków last night. I gave the collected poems typescript back to Wydawnictwo Literackie. Now I'm sitting at the desk, nearly 7pm. Head empty, finding it difficult to breathe. I would like to spend ten days in the woods at least, in the country... I don't know if I can organise it for myself. Everything's disintegrating for me, even my most modest plans. I can't organise two weeks for myself.

Went to Mother in hospital; she looks slightly better. I cannot organise my work. Sluggish and tired. In October I shall be 36. I cannot work; this is horrible. I can't think. Will I wake up? I live in a dream. What am I doing, then? What am I?

I feel worn out. I'm falling apart, over and over. Something is falling apart, falling down. I can't free myself; I am locked up, I have been locked up, somebody locked me up, I locked me up. My life consists of spasmodic awakenings and the daily grind – as though it got scarred twenty years ago and snapped in half. I am an equable madman, a proud worm, a calm troublemaker – I love forests and the country but I'm stuck in Silesia spending entire Junes, Julys and Augusts locked in this room poring over a few scribbled sheets of paper.

In our final conversation Staff said to me, 'It is useless squeezing yourself in... it even affects the writing, it has a negative impact.' I've come to understand him – I'm the living proof.

30 JUNE 1957, SUNDAY

The heatwave has reached 40°C. I tried to work.

Weak, ponderous.

I'm supposed to collect Mother from hospital tomorrow.

Henryk V. – I have been reading his book *Escape from the Abyss*. The man lives, works, loves, has a wife and a child. When he was in the camp, for a period he was with the *Leichenkommando*, burying corpses and those still living who were thrown into the pit. Henryk is a good man. I'm running round my so-called study with a newspaper, killing big black horseflies. Cursing my work, dripping sweat, and can do nothing.

A note in the old paper: 'What is virtue? The French critic Emil Herriot recently gave a talk at the Académie Française on the notion of "virtue". He quoted a definition by Stendhal: "Virtue is the ability to carry out acts which are detrimental to oneself but necessary for the happiness of others".'

All the years I've worked in Poland I've never known the possibility of expressing myself: the reason being that I'm not and never have been linked to a publication. I bring out pieces on a casual basis and that's all I do. Whereas I would need some corner of my own, however small, to be able to express myself freely. Editors have always had a strange attitude to me. I had many interesting subjects, issues I wanted to probe – still have, but where? I can't even get access to the provincial weeklies.

I have always been dependent on the whims of poetry 'editors', and the other editors; I've published a lot, but how did it happen?

Meanwhile – after the days when they treated me like rubbish (1950-1953 – my 'generation' particularly excelled at it, each and every mediocrity mentored me and clipped me round the ear), I was gagged and had no chance to reply. Now one of the cynics is chief editor of *Nowa Kultura*. I'm chucked out again; obviously I can send stuff to miscellaneous magazines, but that's all.

I have no openings. I'm as tied up as ever. The literary pimp cliques are still in action... This time they're pretending to be 'revolutionaries' – moralists – reformers. People believe moral degenerates like Ważyk are the precursors of the Polish October. Maybe one day I'll find the time and strength to tell the whole truth about these frauds with typewriters. It's a gang without a structure, they support themselves, promote themselves... Obviously they all stink the same.

The nauseating slurry that half drowned me for so many years – mouth, eyes, nose – it's spilling everywhere again: all over the editorials, the unions, the publishers, the radio. 'Regeneration'.

How I survived in that muckheap, no one will ever know. They treated me like a schoolboy sending little verses to the editor – never ever any communication with them, luckily I do not have to look at them, speak to them, 'debate'. How much damage did they do me? Literati, 'moralists', pederasts, *pryszczaci*...

2 JULY 1957

Evening. In the next room mother is whimpering. She held my hand and talked. I brought her over from the hospital yesterday. Who can I get down on my knees to, so she won't suffer so much. At noon it was 36°C. I took Janek, Kamil and Wiesława to Katowice – put them on the train. They went to the country.

How my poor mother suffered all those years after Janusz's death (right until today – this very day) – I cannot think about what the Gestapo did to him.

3 JULY 1957, WEDNESDAY

This morning mother kept losing consciousness, didn't recognise me – kept saying: 'They've all gone somewhere, Janusz, Stasiu, Father.' Swelling water was suffocating her.

Before I left in the morning I massaged her legs and rubbed camphor oil into her back. At some point she said, 'Stupid life.' In the afternoon I called the doctor.

Mother had a little... ice cream. Begged for it like a child. A bit of potatoes and veal for dinner. She wanted her pillows moved, she wants to lie by the window, to see – 'a green garden... the little bird singing.' She wanted me to eat something. 'Are you sure you've eaten?'

'I don't want to be buried in Gliwice here with the Germans; I want to be in... or in Częstochowa... in Częstochowa.'

I went to the fields. Brought back camomile flowers.

The only thing I wish for is a walk in the forest and yet I can't fix it for myself. I can't. After three days... There are tales of heroic people who lock themselves up in a hermitage, renounce *life* in order to work and think – but I, I'm such a wretch that for years I've been dreaming of some cell where I might spend half a year writing quietly. No, that's too much happiness, obviously – I ask for too much, don't I? The worst thing is having to leave her alone with her suffering – because even my presence is exhausting her.

Reading Flaubert's *Letters*.

4 JULY 1957, THURSDAY

This morning mother-in-law came to me, says, 'Go to the shop and buy two candles.' 'What candles, why?' I didn't know what she meant – but instantly it's all clear. When she says, 'The table's prepared, there's water, the cross, your mother's been washed, the priest's on his way, and all that's needed are two candles for two small candlesticks.' I went to mother and mother says, 'I'm a grown-up, I know I have to die,' then, after a moment holding my hand..., 'I want to live so much, a bit longer,' then she explained to me where to find Bankowa Street, 'I feel like some wild strawberries, the village women sell their produce there.' Now the priest is coming for the confession. In the evening I brought the doctor. Mother was in a great deal of pain. We gave her sleeping pills for the night.

Dreadful heat – must be over 40°C in the sun. Flies everywhere.

5 JULY 1957, FRIDAY

Yesterday I asked a nun, Sister Beatrice, to come this morning to give the injection. It's about letting the water out – it's suffocating Mother. I rubbed some oils and spirit into her sides, she has flu-like pains.

She went to the toilet in the night. She wanted to do it by herself, she fell. When I ran in she kept apologising, crying, 'There's no faeces, just some spilt urine.' It's five in the morning – it's heating up again – the sun's shining. It's stifling. There's been a heatwave for two weeks. The nun came at six. It took her fifteen minutes to find a vein, they're so slack, they keep disappearing. Staś and Father have been here for two days. I can hear the doorbell in the hall. The priest has come to Mother with Holy Communion. After Extreme Unction Mother said, 'Tadziu, I feel so good.' Mother has taken Holy Communion, she is praying. The heat gets unbearable around noon. Even this morning it was 30°C in the shade. I'm sat in my room sweating. It's turning into hell outside, you can't breathe, it must be 50°C, and my poor Mother (poor Job) is dying. Should I wish for her death? Let her give me a look at least, say something, make some half-conscious gesture. A cursed time, the hottest July I remember in all my life. At a time like this, not a single cloud in the sky and the cruel sun making my eyes black out. I'd be so happy if she could just live for a few weeks without suffering but it's a happiness I daren't dream of.

7 JULY 1957, SUNDAY

Mother is alive. She can only swallow liquids. Yesterday and today I gave her pessaries with morphine. Mirka and Zosia R. came to visit. Mother talked a bit. About forests. Mother grew up in the woods, spent her childhood in the woods.

Mother moved her hand, when I got closer she started to talk – a whispering, burnt out voice: 'When I was a young girl, I found a tiny spring in the wood between two trees. The water was clear and cold, I used to scoop it with my hand or lie on my tummy and go like this...' Mother put out her tongue and it flickered – like a cat drinking milk from a bowl. She went quiet, after a while she spoke again: 'The woods are beautiful, not like people. When swallows are about to fly away to hot countries, they form a great ball, all round and black, and the ball rises up in the air...' She was silent for a little, then went on, whispered, 'One day I was sitting in the forest and a doe came out from behind the trees and looked around... then she went and fetched her children, two little ones, and stepped across the clearing. And another time I saw a white cloud in the meadow, it was a flock of storks. Nature's so beautiful and they're dropping the Bomb. From tomorrow I must have a rusk in the morning, because I'm all shrunk inside from the hunger and nothing gets through. I'll die of hunger.'

I helped Mother into the armchair. She sat there for a while and then she said: 'We'll go.' I didn't realise, I thought she was saying that one day we'd go somewhere far away, but she was saying 'we'll go' from the armchair to the bed – two steps. Having taken those two steps she lay down on her side in the bed breathless and tired. I promised when she felt stronger I'd take her to the balcony, so she could see the lawn down there.

It rained yesterday, and today it's hot again, over thirty degrees. I'm tired, half asleep.

9 JULY 1957, TUESDAY

Yesterday Aunt F. and Staś's wife arrived. Mother is alive, weaker. She had one rusk. Yesterday I gave her an enema. The thermometers showed fifty degrees in the sun. A thunderstorm in the night. At night I get up, take Mother to the toilet, give her some water, adjust her pillows. I can hear every noise. I'm instantly awake. Mirka and Auntie asked which church Wiesława and I married in.

Mirka left Mother a cross from Rome, it's supposed to grant pardons or something. Auntie said we ought to order a Mass in Jasna Góra – she seized the chance to tell me about a miracle she witnessed. A lame man rose and began to walk – I don't remember exactly because I wasn't listening. Auntie said we should write to Father Marian to come.

Father left. I'm tired.

It's cooled down today. Slight relief. Nights are the worst.

She's in the other room, breathes, whimpers, but she's alive! Alive.

10 JULY 1957, WEDNESDAY

Only got up a few times in the night. Mother had a reasonable night. In the morning I looked for soda water, she likes it. She had a gall bladder attack. She can't move by herself. Staś is in Gliwice. Zosia arrived at night at 21:30 and brought Mother a live chicken from Wieluń. She had to leave at 22:00. Bad connections, she'll be travelling all night.

I bought Conrad's *Typhoon* and *The Forester* by Maria Kuncewiczowa. There is some great force in Mother that will not let her die.

It's cooler today.

I stopped writing the Staff memoir a month ago.

I enjoyed reading what Céline says in *L'Express*. About technique and writing a novel, an honest interesting statement: 'In *Journey* I still make concessions to "good literature". You can still find a well-turned phrase there. I think, from the point of view of technique, it's a bit old-fashioned...'

It's so good to read what you've been thinking yourself, as far back as 1945-47, doing poetry (I've such pieces in *Anxiety*).

L'Express: 'What do you expect from your new book?'

Céline: 'I expect an advance from Gallimard, that's all, nothing else... When I get it, I'll find a little cubbyhole in the country and finish the book. I won't write any more... If they paid me the lot, I wouldn't bother publishing it. I'd give up mixing that muck...'

12 JULY 1957, FRIDAY

Four in the morning. I left mother a second ago. I put her on the toilet, adjusted the pillows, all night she never slept. I carried her, she was whimpering. At four I woke Staś – we moved Mother into the armchair, we changed her sheets. Whimpering all night: 'Why am I alive'... Desperate, tired, irritated, I answered 'I don't know,' there was a moment I would have shouted at her – how weak is a man? Evil? There's a fly circling the lit lamp. You can hear distant trains – engines. The damned fly won't even let me write these few words.

12 JULY 1957, FRIDAY

I confused the dates. The night with mother.

Mother talks less and less, utters fewer and fewer words: as if she were losing her words. Sometimes she speaks very unclearly, mumbling almost, especially when she's just woken. Her most frequent words: 'air, water, burns, hurts'. She's communicating through glances and signs. The doctor came yesterday. Last night Mother didn't sleep. She keeps waking. A baby's babbling gives rise to words of life – the babblings of someone departing signify a fading away, decay, the disintegration of words leading to the final silence. She is a sick little child.

13 JULY 1957, SATURDAY

Mother like a bird – sips water, eats a few crumbs of a rusk and it's like that all day, but she has no strength to lift her head, move a leg. You have to put her on the toilet: it's painful for her. From the morning, bile was escaping from her. She asks to be pulled up gently.

I spent an hour in the field today. The harvest's coming. I never noticed it when summer arrived.

Yesterday a card came from P. They'll get the funding for their *Rzecz* magazine. It's like hearing and reading about last year's snow. Today a letter from F. and a postcard from Kornel, on a canoe expedition. Lucky man! Unhappy in some way, though, known only to him. Keeps himself close.

Now it's evening. Coming up to nine. Through the window you can hear footsteps, faint bird voices. Mum doesn't speak. Doesn't listen when I read to her. She wakes as if returning to things unknown, but she is still conscious, neat, clean. My old lady is so brave.

We sent a parcel to the country. Yesterday I sent Wiesława some newspapers. It's cooler – at least that's a grace. Staś mentions he'd like to go to Łódź for a day or two.

The birch tree behind the window is green. Summer 1957.

In 1954 I started to write a story, 'The Sea' – and then three years' break. I tried again before the trip to Paris. I've stopped trying. I put it in the drawer. It's dark now in my room.

14 JULY 1957, SUNDAY

Five in the afternoon. Rain. A gall bladder attack stopped a moment ago – bile came out of mother for almost an hour. 'The stones are crushing me' – she points to her chest indicating that's where the stones are. 'Tadziu, son, help me, I can't breathe.' I pass her a jar, a reeking yellow fluid flows into it from her mouth, Staś and I rearrange the pillows a hundred times. Her legs are heavy, feet swollen; unable to move, she asks us to sit her up: 'Higher, I can't breathe.' She only had two spoonfuls of chicken soup today. Her skull is covered in bluish-yellowish skin, almost translucent. She hates the bedpan. She's so weak she can't support herself with her elbows. We put a suitcase by her legs – so she has something to press against. It's raining. I'm sitting in my room.

I wanted to read mother a few poems but she's drifting asleep; she's weakening. Besides, the poems sounded alien – so remote.

I stopped. 'Water, air, can't breathe, higher…' They're about the only words left.

Moving into the armchair is now an expedition. Getting up higher on the pillows is an adventure. A long preparation as if for a journey. It's raining. People are walking to the Cinema Aurora. My city? The city I've lived in since 1950. What connects me to it? Nothing. It's raining.

The two principal thoughts that have preoccupied me for weeks: get a haircut, get my shoes repaired... oh, and then there's emptiness, darkness, fear. Of what? Expectation. Of what?

Where's this whole spiritual sphere? 'There is torment of the body, barrenness, tears.' Where's the 'soul' hiding, then? When does it appear, when does it vanish? What kind of action is the writing of poems? What is it?

I suspect nobody actually knows.

The worst poem can be a good poem – for somebody, sometime, somewhere... So why do you correct the text ten times over... What, who demands that? What's the force at work inside a poet, writing?

The gall bladder attack is still going on.

It's as if she's completely emptied herself. Her poor tiny bones. Staś said, 'I wish Mother would die.' I can't bring myself to second his wish – the best thing one could hope for her.

An unclear poem.

The Seine doesn't exist. There's only... There's no Eiffel Tower. There's no Paris. There's a mouth.

16 JULY, 1957, TUESDAY

1 o'clock at night – Mother is dying. 'Take me.' It's 10 o'clock in the morning, Mother hasn't died yet. It started pouring. Neither Father nor Staś has arrived yet. 'Take me, take me, mummy' – she reached out her hands, not to me. Mother died at 10:20 in the morning. *Carcinoma ventriculi.*

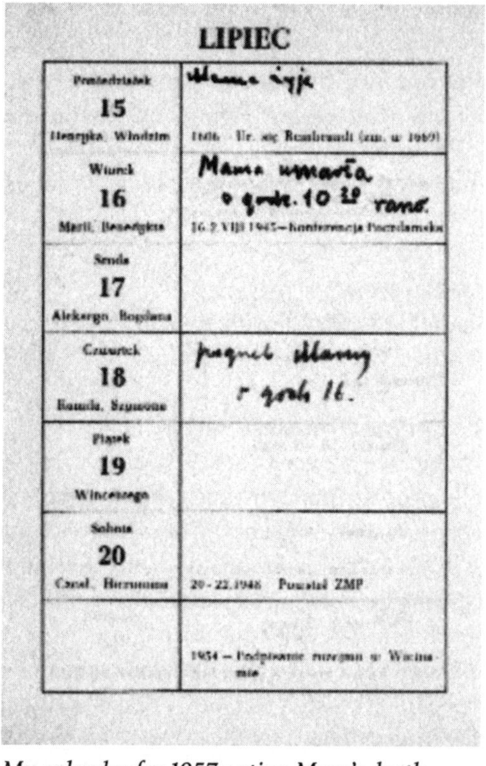

My calendar for 1957 noting Mum's death

17 JULY 1957

Staś and I have bought a coffin, a cheap simple pine coffin. Mother is lying in the bedroom in the coffin, beneath a sheet. It's rained since the morning. Funeral tomorrow.

19 JULY 1957

Yesterday at four we buried Mother. Yesterday the people who came for the funeral left. Father and Staś are due to leave tomorrow. I'll be left alone.

I returned my darling to the earth. My good suffering child – my soul.

20 JULY 1957, SATURDAY

Staś and Father left today. I'm sitting alone in the room, in my 'study'. It's quiet. Mum I am talking and will always be talking to you.

I'll talk to you as if you were next to me.

There was a funeral service at 6:30 today. During the service I was kneeling and not praying, repeating after the priest... Hail Mary, full of grace... after all I haven't prayed for almost twenty years. The priest in his black chasuble sang 'Rest in peace' for you. Your grave's in a little cemetery: there are fields all round and two big chestnut trees by the grave. There's a small plaque on the cross with your first name and your surname – and the inscription: 'She asks, sigh to God' – Staś and I dictated the words to the undertaker.

Mummy my love, you're by my side. I shall be talking to you, I'll work thinking of you. Of your faint kind smile on a terribly gaunt yellow face – when you slipped away. My Good Beloved Old Lady, it's hard to breathe. But I am writing this like a letter to you. You were my trepidation, fear, joy and breath. I'm kissing your parched hands and swollen legs, dearest, your eyes – your blue hands as you died. I'm kissing your agonised body, which I gave back to our great mother – the earth.

21 JULY 1957, SUNDAY

The first Sunday without Mother. I tried to do something. But I can't. It's raining. It's late morning, dark and empty. My factory town. I might go to the train station to read the timetable, I might go for a stroll past the delicatessen, go past three, four, churches, I might look at the drunks and the motorcyclists, at...

'You will fly with them to the hot countries, where you will know no snow, cold or hunger, and every year you will leave us here, always waiting... for you... longing for you as the heralds of spring, and we shall wait, also, until death takes us each by surprise, but in the meanwhile, dear nightingale, sing us the sad tunes...'

Wolica, 4 May 1857

(K. Wodzicki, *Ornithological Notes*)

Winter passed, spring passed, summer 1957 is passing. When will I get down to 'work'?

Mummy my Love. I lost the game because I had to lose, unhappy and absurd.

22 JULY 1957

Dearest Mummy, this is Monday. I am at home. I was in the garden this morning. It's cloudy today. I'm not working. I read a bit. I'm tired. Perhaps I shall go on holiday. But at this moment – at the end of the summer – I couldn't say where to. I know I should get down to work, time flies. It's running away.

But just a moment, let's talk a little longer. My Good Beloved Old Lady. I'm kissing your hands and your eyes.

I'm talking to You.

a page torn from a diary

27 JUNE 1982, SUNDAY

[...]

It was 7 o'clock. It rained. I looked in the calendar. Today is St Władysław's Day. Father's name day. On Father's name day we used to give him a handmade card called a *laurka*, with a picture of flowers, a special verse for the occasion, and sometimes we would recite the verse. Mum dressed us up that day. I remember being incredibly shy when it was my turn to say the poem. I was such a shy child. When anyone talked about me in my presence I wished the earth would swallow me up and I could vanish. We were on holiday once... I could have been three, certainly it was long before school and my first communion. We visited Father Michnikowski's parish where Mother spent some time as a little girl, we were invited out to eat. I remember a long table in a dining room, there were many people there. I was at the table with my older brother Janusz. Staś wasn't born yet. I remember being so shy. I whispered into Mother's ear to be allowed to sit with my back to everyone, so they wouldn't see me... Miss Emilia, the priest's housekeeper, found it very amusing. They did finally put me on a chair with my back to the faces of the others at the table, and a bowl of soup was set in front of me on another chair. Eating the soup was torture, I remember. Miss Emilia's hair was tied in a bun. In her room she had cats and little bowls and saucers of milk. My brother and I sat on the floor looking at big illustrated newspapers. There were black line drawings and photographs on shiny smooth paper. It was the *Tygodnik Ilustrowany*...

...twenty years later

MUM YOU RECOGNISE ME... a smile on the tiny ravaged face, translucent skin grey hair on her head – yes of course son it's you
Mum it's me please have the borscht swallow a few more spoonfuls –
mouth closed and red nutritious borscht drips sideways stains the chin I wipe her face diminished face
with a hanky and bring the spoon up again to her closed mouth Mum is sitting on her bed with her back against the pillows... through the window you can see the Russian vine the light through translucent leaves Mum wants to look out the window beyond the window the red walls of some warehouses bakery military hospital

Now I'm in the country seventeen years later I forgot the anniversary of Your death I had a visit from a friend a theatre director we spent hours talking it was a hot day we walked through the woods to some shallow lakes the sweat dripped down my neck my back one hot July like this I threw a handful of earth on your wooden coffin a dog is running ahead of us panting snatches a thick stick goes berserk splashing water sun-warmed water silted with slime warmed-up covered with bulrushes the blue elongated azure lines are dragonflies over the surface of the water a crater healed and filled again I went to the cemetery this year to Your grave turned earth inside a cement frame a few withering yellowish flowers the poor gravestone fake stone I was on my way from a foundry a massive building site springing up in Silesia near Dąbrowa Górnicza

thirty thousand builders five thousand crew the driver who took me from the hotel to the construction site and the canteen was young and helpful we talked about work and life

I notice there are fewer and fewer butterflies in the world and
my mind wakes from an oppressive dream the rain is falling
on us on the surface of the earth the scent of the woods the rye
and you under the earth under the earth? You go deeper
up here on the earth I listen to music and by means of eyes and
hands my brain transfers the shape of my thoughts into letters
I've been thrashed around since the morning
I'm thrashing on the surface like straw
give me the grace of inner concentration let me see. It's been
years. You're gripping my hands my legs you pull me into the
earth I denied you the Cock crows as I wake
I'm kneeling by the bed but I'm not praying I've shut my eyes
It's been five six seven months since I started to write *Clearing*
a few sentences and then a break filled with what? With life.
That's to say... music Ravel
Sonatine in green birds' voices drown the music from the radio
July
approaching the 20th anniversary of Your death. That murmur
is the raindrops
rain
the music in the rustling – and I alive

evening coming

sin

WE'RE ONE BODY. Can't you feel it?

We know nothing about each other.

I've already told you everything. Life's not made up of extraordinary things. I won't talk about the War.

Talk about you, just you.

Me? Fine, I will tell you about one strange event. In all my life I've never experienced fear like that. Such temptation, such terror. I was eight at the time...

There weren't many beautiful objects in our house. On the table in the big room there was an artillery gilza.

A 'gilza'?

It could be a technical term, I don't know... it was an empty cannon shell. We called it 'the gilza'. It was copper. There was a cap underneath with a dent from the firing pin. It came from a spent shell back in WWI. I always confuse copper and brass, we called *grosz* coins coppers even though they must have been brass. In the winter the gilza was full of tissue paper flowers. It wasn't till about ten years after the First War that mum bought a larger mirror, an oval one. For years the only mirror we had in the house was a little square thing. Hanging in the kitchen. She bought a big extendable table then too. There wasn't any sunlight in the main room. It was always shady. I can't remember the trees anymore but there were trees, growing in front of the house. In the evening, mother darned socks and stockings. Sometimes father sat down with the paper. There was an oil lamp on the table. It was bright at the table but all the corners of the room were dark. Shadows moved on the walls. Huge hands, heads.

One day I noticed there was a vase in the room. It looked like a massive egg. I didn't notice the gilza, I forgot all about it.

Now the whole room was filled by the vase. I went closer to the table, studied the vase. It was white. Filled with light at the top and almost transparent. But its belly was fat, shiny. I reached out my hand. I heard mother's footsteps and my hand dropped. Mother asked with a smile, 'It's nicer now, isn't it? Just don't touch it, don't touch it! It's a porcelain vase. Father may be cross I've bought it. But the room's nicer now.'

'What will go in it? Flowers?'

'No,' mother said, 'it isn't for flowers.'

'Then what is it for?'

'Nothing. It's beautiful in itself, has such a beautiful shape, it's decorative in itself. Only please, don't touch it.'

'Why?'

'Mustn't touch beautiful things,' mother said and left the room.

I stood there for a while staring at the porcelain vase. It was the first beautiful thing in our flat that didn't serve some purpose. There were chairs, pans, plates, spoons, buckets, pictures, beds, tables, but all those objects had their uses. Even the gilza used to be a cannon shell. But this beautiful vase had no function. It had never been anything else. It wasn't even a vase, come to that. Because we mustn't fill it with water or put flowers in it. It was beautiful in itself. Without flowers. Mother had never mentioned she was going to buy such a vase. With the mirror or the new table there were discussions for months. But the vase popped up out of the blue. Like an egg abandoned by some unknown gigantic bird.

One day I was at home alone... Aren't you listening?

I am.

... I stood by the table staring at the vase. Then I reached out my hand. The vase had a cool surface. And the room was warm. I remember best the light and the vase. The light in the room was like the light in the crown of a huge thick tree. Damp as in a well, greenish, vivid. As if water were flowing through the walls. There standing in that light was the vase. My fingers touched it. Gently I stroked its cold surface. I placed my hand, felt the swell, roundness. I had in my hand the shape of beauty. I held my hand like that for a long while and I could feel the surface of the vase growing warmer. I pulled my hand away from the vase and I went into the kitchen where I kept my soldiers in a box under the table. I arranged them in their ranks. But I didn't enjoy it. I chucked the army in the box and went back to the room. I put my ear to the vase and tapped gently. I wasn't alone in the room, I was with a vase who was a stranger in our flat. It decorated the room but didn't do anything. All the objects, furniture, pictures were connected with us and with one another by invisible threads. Like veins blood flows through. Day and night. Whereas the vase was alone. Cut off from everything. Was it really beautiful? To me it was mysterious, alien. Not of our flat. The feeling I had for it was like the feelings of a primitive man worshipping an idol. A miraculous idol that had plummeted from the sky. First it was untouchable. But it was becoming beautiful too. I can see mother's face as she said, 'Isn't the vase beautiful?' And when she spoke to Father later that same day she said, 'It decorates the flat better than the loveliest piece of furniture.' What father said to this, I don't recall.

Winter arrived. Warmth came from an iron stove where the peat burnt day and night. Puddles were covered with panes of ice. We threw stones at them or kicked them with our hobnailed boots. The ice cracked and became covered with something that looked like spreading white hairs. It crunched crisply under our hooves. One day I had a sore throat and didn't go to school. I was in bed, reading *Mucha*... it was a comic... printed on pink paper. Not pink exactly but turning towards a pinkish shade. On the face of it I was looking through *Mucha,* but in my mind's eye I saw the vase on the table. It stood there, alien, perfect, untouchable. Carefully, slowly, I went on tiptoe although nobody was home. I moved stealthily in a silence in which the vase stood as if in cotton wool. I pulled at the tablecloth, the vase moved. Then I pulled a little more strongly. The vase swayed and toppled. There were papers on the table. The vase rolled for a few centimetres and stopped at the table edge. Inside there was a bluish light. I knew what would happen next. I was so scared. I actually began to pray: 'Guardian Angel stand by me, Angel of God I call on thee. Morning, evening, night and day, Be near to bring me help I pray.' But something tempted me and I pulled the tablecloth again. Now I don't believe it anymore, but at that time and that place the Devil turned up, the Devil took my hand, and tugged. I really didn't mean it. I could still catch the vase at the last moment, because it was turning slowly, as if on its axis, and then it was very slowly falling to the floor. It fell so slowly, I could have caught it in the air... but the Devil held my hands. I'm laughing too now. But it was the one and only time the Devil tempted me. Afterwards I always sinned on my own account...

1963

the resit

I REMEMBER my religion teacher. She was a cheerful corpulent lady with shiny black eyes, black hair, a dark complexion and unusually white teeth. I remember her surname. Mrs Kryszczyńska. She taught me religion, the catechism, and prepared me for my First Communion. It was 1928. There was poverty around, a foretaste of the massive unemployment approaching. So what did it matter if I earned a five, the top mark, in religion. We couldn't afford a new outfit. You can't go to First Communion in your everyday school clothes. Mum decided I would go next year. This was a disaster. I sobbed terribly. And then as usual Mum found the solution. We had the white outfit at home that Januszek wore for his First Communion three years earlier; it needed freshening up and altering slightly. This meant that now we only needed white stockings, shoes and a candle... I still snivelled quietly though it was sorted out. However, first of all one had to go to Confession, the sacrament of penance. The conscience exam wasn't difficult. The list of sins wasn't too long: Impurity. Gluttony. Greed. Sloth. Lying. Anger. My first confessor was Father Peakcap. Actually his real name was Father Bielawski but when we were children nearly everyone had a nickname, not exactly pseudonyms but names we made up, and often adults did that too. This priest used to wear a navy-blue flat-topped peaked cap, hence the nickname. So I was required to examine my conscience. As it was my very first confession it concerned my entire eight-year-old life. Most space was taken up by such sins as lying, sloth, greed – and impurity in thought, word and deed. There were terms like 'immodest looks and words,' and 'dirty games'. I was very devout. I said most of my prayers to Lord Jesus as he knelt in the Garden of Gethsemane. In my mind I called this

Lord Jesus 'God with the fat tummy' until I looked closer at the picture, and realised God was kneeling by a rock with his robe hanging over it, which looked like a big belly. I fasted on Friday, only ate dry bread and drank water. Our older cousin Zosia Rajsówna aka 'The Needle' called me 'our little saint'. Of course the little saint like all saints had his frailties and sins... sometimes he ate pork scratchings or a bit of sausage on a Friday, sometimes he had impure thoughts when he saw dogs mating in the street or a cock yanking at a hen in the yard... greed... included raisins plucked from a cake, eating sugar from the sugar bowl, a 10-grosz cube of halva... I made my confession, I received absolution and penance... five Our Fathers and five Hail Marys... That night, I felt thirsty and I had two or three sips of water... then I couldn't sleep, I was so worried, had I just sinned? In the morning I decided I must resit the exam before my First Communion, I was so tormented by doubts... but Father Peakcap dispelled them with a gesture and a smile.

Sins were all sorts of trouble. As the years passed the sins changed, ballooned, assumed different shapes and colours. Like the vowels in Rimbaud's poem... black A – white E – red I... Carrying his eighth cross in his eighth decade, an old man returns to the sins of his childhood... greed gluttony drunkenness sloth and impurity... I let down my cousin Needle and failed to become a little saint... and I don't know if I shall ever take the resit.

Now as I write these words, Mother's eyes are on me. In her eyes there is a question she never asked.

[the way home from school]

[a fragment from a letter]

Janusz Różewicz

RADOMSKO, 25 MAY 1940

[...]
The day began with white lilies of the valley... This means
it is my name day today. You see it's been years since I started
to find lilies of the valley that day lying across my quilt in the
morning. Sometimes it's jasmine. But this year the jasmine has
not yet blossomed... Now I am sitting at my desk thinking about
myself. I think it's right to devote an hour once a year to thinking
about such an important person as Mr Janusz Różewicz.

[...]
the green surface of the desk at which I'm sitting – bright
shining saturated with sunlight – there are sixteen desks like
it in the classroom

the desks in the corners – darker – because in the shade –
all this is terribly
simple... through the window it's also green. but different – the
green of this table and the green of the branches are two quite
different colours although they share the one name – green...

the last lesson – you rush quickly out from the dark
corridor – your bag isn't even heavy... shoes clatter
on the pavement's grey cement squares...
the rapid stream of navy-blue hats and uniforms
berets and black pinafores has already flooded by
leaving only scattered latecomers, walking fast
and disappearing around the corner

and on that corner – attached to the fence
a display case filled with kino photographs says that today
at three
'especially for the young...' everything this week
is especially for the young... the foremost and the nicest (or
possibly simply the last?) week of study...
the tall white cinema like the belly of a transatlantic
liner stays behind us... in the street to the right
one of the pretty little houses of our French colony – on the
balcony
a lot of boxes with petunias...
I walk under chestnut trees whose shadows fall on the convent
wall
shadows of heavy branches on the pavement separated by gold
strips of sunshine – bookshop windows draw the eye
with a coloured crowd of book jackets 'the latest arrivals'...
adjacent to the street a small triangular garden
concrete
is empty – in vain do the black letters on the signs recommend
the 'urban garden to be cared for by the public' –
the dear public is now having lunch
now I'm passing the fire station gates
as usual I am tempted by a small glass pane – to be
broken in the event of an emergency... on the clock
of the town hall it's two...
in a navy-blue uniform and a white cap a policeman is pacing
the crossroads... how do you control traffic that doesn't exist
a newspaper kiosk has tintacks holding up
papers smelling of printer's ink and yesterday's news
heavy crows squat on church towers...
over-excited sparrows debate in the dust of the street...
the green's narrow paths meet under the spiky
agave plant which is the centre of gravity of the whole market
square

Janusz, the elder brother,
after his matriculation

Mum and Zulka, Janusz's girlfriend

our street begins with a red letterbox
(perhaps I'll find a letter waiting at home, well at least the
newspaper...)
everything feels awfully light and it isn't me walking, something
is walking me...
now my shadow is jumping all over the fence – simply the sun's
projections
– of posts, rails and steps... an open window
has panes made of silver, to blind the eyes
I cross to the other side – still two more steps
and here's the gate to my house, it's dark inside
but in the back yard the sun is the same as in the street
up the spiral staircase to the door...

in the kaleidoscope...

Stanisław Różewicz

FOR YEARS at six o'clock: the sirens of the Mazovia and Metalurgia factories, the church bells...

Mum gets up first, lights the stove, makes breakfast before father leaves to catch the train. Father commutes for twenty years to a job in the court in Częstochowa. We get up after mum calls, 'Boys, it's seven...', it's time to get ready for school.

My first encounter with school... We walk down a long corridor, I'm in a little dark velvet uniform, I stand in front of the headmaster, Mr Kupczyński. Mum tells him I learned to read all by myself, which was true, so perhaps I could be admitted to Year Two, skipping a year... The headmaster picks up the newspaper from his desk, makes me read an article on page one. I read fairly fluently but at some point I stumble over a word I don't know: 'counter-revolution'. I go silent, whisper a pathetic lie to mum, that I'm too shy to carry on reading. Mum passes it on to the headmaster, he smiles knowingly: 'That's fine, he'll be accepted'... We walk back happy. Did mum know it was a pathetic trick, did she believe me? She repeats it once, twice: 'counter-revolution'. I follow on softly: 'counter-revolution'... She tries to explain the meaning of the word.

Mum's holding my hand. We're walking. It's December, to meet Santa Claus. The town hall's full of lights and children, seems gigantic to me. The hubbub of voices subsides when Santa comes in. He's followed by two angels carrying a basket packed with presents. The angels call out the children's first and second names, Santa gives out the presents. I get a bag containing new gloves, sweets, and a kaleidoscope. I look into the tube. And hold it up against the light. As I twist, a bright rosette, a star, changes shape inside it, colours rotate, create a new star, there's something magical about it. One day my enchanted kaleidoscope fell apart, and a dozen bits of coloured glass as well as three tiny mirrors spilled out...

First trip with mum to 'theatre'. The Charitable Society Hall, we've come to see the nativity play. Enchanted, I gaze at a star wandering in the sky, at the Shepherds and the Three Kings. I am much impressed by wicked Herod and the Devil yelling, 'King Herod, for your dreadful sins, welcome to Hell and come on in!' Suddenly from behind the throne there emerges the Grim Reaper, all white, carrying a scythe. Frightened and thrilled, I squeeze mum's hand. Mum smiles at me reassuringly. But this image of death with a white face stays with me for long years to come.

I'm older and mum's taking me to The Kinema, the picture-house at the fire station. Through the little window with multicoloured panes you can see the ticket clerk. Mum always buys seats up in the balcony. Before the shows, a boy with a cap goes round spraying everything with Forest Air. The huge chandelier under the ceiling dims and we watch *The Hurricane, The Prince and The Pauper, The Crusades* with Loretta Young. At home, mum always says she preferred the actresses in the old silent films – Asta Nielsen, Lillian Gish and the one who starred in *The Empress of the World*. Out of today's stars she likes Greta Garbo and Jadwiga Smosarska.

Our flat in Długa Street hasn't got a corridor or hall. From outside you come straight into the kitchen. In the winter, snowflakes swirl in when you open the door. One evening a frightened neighbour runs in: 'Come!', she says. Red trails are waving in the sky, tall beams of light moving around, now orange, then light blue, it lasts for ages. I'm seven or eight, I'm terrified, here comes the end of the world... Mum hugs me to her, the curtains in the sky fade slowly, the stars come out... 'It must be a reflection of the Northern Lights,' mum says. *The Express* writes up the extraordinary phenomenon the following day.

The door opens... In comes mum from the rain, with a scarf round her shoulders, crying. They said on the radio that a plane crashed in a storm and Żwirko and Wigura – the pilot and the designer – were killed, only a week after they won the Berlin Challenge. The whole nation was rejoicing, and now...

A Chinese man in a dark coat opens a massive suitcase, tries to persuade mum to buy some incense, various vases, a silk scarf with dragons and exotic birds. I can't remember if mum bought anything, money was tight. I remembered the Chinese man in the dark coat half a century later when I saw inside the Emperor's Palace in Peking as a tourist. Mum never went to the mountains or the sea.

Our new flat in Polska Organizacja Wojskow Street has two rooms and a kitchen and a hall. Father keeps playing the lottery, saying, 'I must win a million.' Mum smiles tolerantly. Winter and summer, a mad lady totters round the back yard. 'O...,' she says over and over, 'Got no devil, got no devil...' Debts and poverty have driven her insane. Her husband, a bricklayer, beats her regularly every week. Bricklayers don't work in the winter. Although we could hardly make ends meet ourselves, mum helps our neighbours the M. family: they used to own a mill, now they're poor, their sons often go hungry. At some point the youngest ran away from home, he saw a miracle in the countryside apparently... 'The apples on a tree turned into pigeons and flew away into the woods...'

Some Sundays we go to the woods in Sucha Wieś, sometimes to somewhere nearer, 'the Acacias' – that's the place past the buildings, in the fields, where we're surrounded by the scent of acacias in blossom. We run as far as the windmill, its wings slowly rotate, they seem to lift us into the sky, we can hear mum calling, she's brought food and drink from home. And Sunday is the day too when visitors come, they often stay for supper, praise mum's cooking, her baking, remember old times.

Father recalls his military service in the Russian army far away in Asia, the murder trial of the monk Damazy Macoch, they talk about Piłsudski's May coup and the strike at the Metalurgia factory. Their old friend Lucia talks about the forest ranger's house haunted by the woman with golden hair. Then they play card games – *tysiąc* or *preferans*. Lots of people come and go, swapping faces: lodgers, neighbours, dinner guests. Adaś R. practises Grieg's 'Aasa's Death' on his violin; Miss Jadzia, the secondary school secretary, laughs with her high voice, she has green eyes. One lodger, Zosia P., lives with us for several years, we like her like a sister, she calls our mother 'Mum'... More and more, there are visits from Janusz's friends – boys and girls – for a name day party or St Andrew's Day. In May we go to St Francis' monastery for May Mass. We pick the first buttercups in the meadow by the River Radomka and take them to mum. Mum loves narcissi and lilacs, all the flowers. On his name day, Janusz always finds lilies of the valley or sometimes jasmine on his bedcovers when he wakes up: that's mum...

Mum is perpetually busy. She cooks, cleans and washes up, mends our clothes, buys our shoes, takes them in for repairs, lights the stove, gets the shopping from the market. Sometimes she sends me to the little shop for some borscht, for tinder fragrant with resin, one or two bundles of wood, lamp oil. Come Christmas, mum does a big clean, polishes the floors, irons and hangs the net curtains, wipes dust off all the furniture, off the alabaster Polish eagle breaking its chains... Father, as per tradition, buys the Christmas tree. From time to time Father brings home strange objects and imitation bronze sculptures materialise – Diana and Venus, a tiger – on the shelves of our *étagère*. From the top of the wardrobe we take down the toy box, mum sticks together a coloured paper chain, we help... Mum loves to sew and embroider, so scissors, needles and coloured

Mayday picnic with Mum.
Left to right: Staś; Marian, Staś' friend, a future
priest; Pulek Ciesielski

threads appear. The big table, the bedside tables and the plant stands are covered with runners and tablecloths big and small, all mum-made. She learned embroidery at an early age when she attended the 'housekeeping courses for girls' on Mr Kozarski's estate in Konopnica. The most beautiful tablecloth in our house is created before my eyes: the white linen blooms with blue, yellow and purple pansies. Mum sometimes croons a song while she's embroidering, 'A month has passed, the dogs have gone to sleep...' Mum reads a lot, in her youth it was Kraszewski and Rodziewiczówna. Later it's Prus, Kaden, Tuwim and Makuszyński, *My Mother's Town* by Boy and *The Story of San Michele*. The books Janusz brings home. When mum has a headache she takes 'those powders with the little rooster on the packet' and puts slices of lemon on her forehead. On a day like that she has tired eyes and speaks with a quiet voice. Later valerian appears. And a doctor, Mr Postolko. Pink, fragrant and the picture of health.

Our behaviour at school doesn't cause mum too much trouble. We're good at the 'arts'; well, we're all three of us hopeless at maths... There are problems covering the school fees at the private *gymnasium*. But mum always comes back smiling from parents' evenings. The form tutor Mr Przyłubski, who teaches Polish, always praises Janusz for his essays and for making speeches at all the official school occasions. Mum's happy when Janusz gets his first things published: 'Janusz was born with a silver spoon in his mouth'... We wanted to know what the spoon looked like.

After the school year it's the holidays, two months in Gabrielów, the village Father's from. Before we go, mum buys us new sandals, packs all the clothes and underwear into a basket. A bus journey to Pajęczno, where our relative Piotr Janik's waiting, then we carry on with him in a cart. Piotr urges on the grey horse, the cart rolls along the sandy road between the fields and the woods. Piotr says what's been happening

And here is the family
(left to right): Father, Staś, Mum, Tadzio,
Miss Zosia P. and Janusz

Father was a dashing cavalier

on his farm and in the village. And here it is, a whitewashed cottage with a red plate saying *Sołtys – Headman –* at the end of the village near the woods. Here comes Jadzia welcoming us, Staś and Sabina running. The familiar coolness and smell of the kitchen, and the other room with the clock and the mirror. We run to say hello to the river. The Warta's clean and full of fish, it rolls with a roar past the mill. We try to drown Sabina to stop her pestering us...

The cousin we call 'The Needle' is in Gabrielów too, and her sister, gentle Antola with the dark eyes, and Uncle Anton with the big moustache, who never stops joking... Mum's favourite place on the river is 'the Valley', a gentle hollow full of fragrant herbs, flowers and bright butterflies. It is only in the holidays that mum takes any rest.

She grew up in the woods. She shows us which mushrooms are good, which are poisonous; she knows everything there is to know about flowers, plants, trees, herbs... Jadzia bakes the bread, we get hot pancakes with butter. A country day lasts twice as long as in town, it gets extinguished slowly, you can hear the sizzling sound of swallows falling into the nests under the thatch. We sleep in the barn on top of the hay, at dawn the sun peeks in through gaps in the planks, sometimes the rain beats down, after the rain the trees and bushes are wet, the air oozes scent. Mum is sitting reading at the edge of the woods. We turn up with potfuls of the black and blue berries we've picked, we play at 'selling' them... Marczak our neighbour brings the fish. Mum takes us to the nearby church in Osjaków where she was christened, we visit the wooden building in Father Michnikowski's parish where she spent quite some time. There's Mrs Miłkowska, there's the cats, there's *Tygodnik Ilustrowany...* We look at the photos.

August is coming to an end, the heather is already in blossom. Tadeusz left a few days early, tomorrow Piotr's taking me and mum to the bus. I run to say goodbye to the river, walk through 'the Valley'. In the shade of hazel trees, there are soldiers lying on the ground. Red faces, exhausted, heads on the earth, some asleep. A freshly dug trench is camouflaged with branches. You can hear a plane circling high above. Across the river, a quiet landscape all the way to the dark stretch of woods on the horizon. Near to the German border. Back home I tell mum about the soldiers and the trench. Mum sighs, 'And what about Janusz...' Janusz has graduated from officer cadet school.

A few days later war broke out. The second day of the war: in the morning we're wishing mum all the best on her name day, a siren sounds the alarm, mum packs things into the basket. Yesterday the first bombs fell on Radomsko. A family friend has arrived, a farmer, he'll take us into the countryside, the town is dangerous. Now we're already in the country. Tadeusz and Zosia are to join us later. I'm standing with mum in front of the house, dark Heinkel aircraft seem to be coming our way, unnaturally slowly. Mum's troubled eyes, Tadeusz and Zosia are in town, we can't warn them... Minutes later, loud explosions from around Radomsko like someone tipping potatoes, dark smoke clouds on the horizon. Tadeusz and Zosia reached us that evening, the airstrike caught them when they were already in the fields, past the old cemetery.

At night the sky is a flaming glow, we're in the column of runaways (running, where?): carts, cyclists. Off the road a side lane into the woods, above the woods white and red flares, we're riding in a wooden cart, dozing. At dawn the wood opens up, bright fog hovers silently over the meadows and the purple heath. A village, Świerczyna. We find a corner in a room packed with refugees. Mum's by the stove boiling the milk. We go back to town two weeks later, you can still smell the burning in the air. Shops looted, houses in the main square and the neighbouring streets ripped apart by the bombs. Our flat's a little looted. All the crockery and the bedding's gone. Mum is sorriest about the green album with the family photos.

The Occupation. Poverty, evil times, horrible. Mum worries, fears for everyone. Sometimes she goes to the country. The tablecloths, the painting, the tapestry go there with her in exchange for a scrap of food, flour, cereal. I spot mum's first grey hair, 'I'll pull it out...', mum smiles: 'Oh, my child...' In autumn 1942 we move out to Częstochowa, we take over a little house in a suburb. From the road you can see the tower of the Jasna Góra monastery, with the blue light at the top at night. A few days after we leave Radomsko, news comes that the Gestapo raided our flat in P.O.W. Street. Here in the little garden in the Parkitka district, mum plants beans, vegetables, the cherry trees and the sweet cherry trees blossom in the spring. She's sown forget-me-nots and nasturtiums under the windows. The little garden makes mum so happy, as though providing protection and a barrier from the main square and the streets where the Germans are rounding up and killing people. Mum's tears after General Sikorski's death... An evening like a portent of approaching freedom: far-off thunder, we're stood in front of the house, the sky and the earth lit up by flares, Christmas tinsel hanging in the sky, the low sound of planes. The Americans are bombing targets in Silesia, a few planes have reached as far as Częstochowa. I watch mum's face staring into the roaring rusted sky...

The last months of the Occupation are very difficult. Mum has more grey hairs, the letters from Janusz stopped in June, she's anxious. Tadeusz and I already know: there was a bust in Łódź, the Gestapo investigated Janusz, he's in prison. We do not tell mum, we tell her tales about all the different situations in the underground when you have to disappear for a long while. A woman who worked with Janusz in the underground later remembered: 'A few days before his arrest, Janusz suddenly said out of the blue – as if anticipating what was to happen – "Above all I'm sorry for my mother...".'

One grey November day, suddenly – who knows how they got in – the house is teeming with military police. They turn it all upside down, search every corner, even behind General Kościuszko's portrait. Where, they ask, were we at such and such a time, who else is staying with us? Tadeusz just came back from his partisan group, there's Wiesława too, she had to escape from Radomsko: they went to town only two hours ago. The police are leafing through books, emptying the wardrobe. Mum is calm, slightly pale. The same thought connects us, that Tadeusz and Wiesława may return at any moment with their fake papers, bad news... Before either of us speaks, mum goes outside past the gate to send them back. We're in luck, the police have wound up and gone. Tadeusz and Wiesława return one hour later.

A cold January, snow. The torrent of the Wehrmacht on the road, retreating. Over towards the town you can see Stukas diving, hear the explosions. There are smoke towers rising, from burning tanks hit by the fighters. The Russians have already broken through into the town. Through the window at dusk you can just make out isolated groups of Germans fleeing on the road. There are military policemen with bazookas in front of the house, a few minutes later they go away too. It is already evening when three young men in Luftwaffe uniforms walk in, exhausted, unshaven. How far are the Russians, I ask. One German waves his hand in resignation, '*Noch weit...*', and to mum, '*Trinken...*', he repeats, '*Trinken*'. In mum's eyes there is neither fear nor hate. She makes them *kawa zobożowa*, coffee from grains, gives it to them. They drink, collapse on the floor by the window, asleep. As if in a delirium, we do not sleep that night. Dawn: suddenly there's shooting nearby, explosions, the three spring up, run out, dissolve in the grey snow and the fog.

Mum departed from us in a town that used to be called Gleiwitz, and is now Gliwice. Sometimes I think of going and seeing Lututów, the little place where mum was born in 1896, a hundred years ago.

Whatever was dearest and most beautiful in our home, was Mum.

about the author

TADEUSZ RÓŻEWICZ (b. 1921) is Poland's foremost living writer. Remarkable for his simultaneous mastery of poetry, prose and drama, he has been nominated for the Nobel Prize for Literature. Tadeusz Różewicz has been translated into over forty languages. The most recent English-language volumes, *recycling* (2001), *New Poems* (2007) and *Sobbing Superpower* (2011), were finalists for the 2003 Popescu Prize (UK), the 2008 National Book Critics Award (USA) and the 2012 Griffin Prize (Canada) respectively. In 2007 he was awarded the European Prize for Literature.

about the translator

BARBARA BOGOCZEK (aka Basia Howard) is a translator and interpreter based in London. She began translating when she was a student in Wrocław in the 1980s, with the cult New Orleans novel *A Confederacy of Dunces* by John Kennedy Toole (published by Wydawnictwo Dolnośląskie, and later reissued by Świat Książki). Since moving to the UK she has worked closely with the poet Ewa Lipska, translating three collections of poetry and – most recently – Lipska's extraordinary novel *Sefer* (AU Press, 2012). She has also had a strong working relationship with Tadeusz Różewicz, publishing his poetry (ARC) and drama (Marion Boyars). These translations were collaborations with Tony Howard, with whom Barbara has also translated the work of Maria Pawlikowska-Jasnorzewska (Wydawnictwo

Literackie) and other Polish poets. She often works in theatre, e.g. co-adapting Bulgakov's *Master and Margarita* (Menier Chocolate Factory), and with the Polish Cultural Institute. She is a legal interpreter (APCI, NRPSI). She is also a member of the Translators Association/Society of Authors. Her current projects include Polish classic children's poetry, Polish fiction, and new work by Ewa Lipska. Her translations have appeared in the *New York Times* and on the London Underground.

about the editor

TONY HOWARD is Professor of English and Comparative Literature at Warwick University. He has collaborated with Barbara Bogoczek on translations of Polish poetry, prose and drama by Tadeusz Różewicz, Ewa Lipska, Maria Pawlikowska-Jasnorzewska, and many others, and edited Różewicz's selected plays: *Reading the Apocalypse in Bed*. His writing on the politics of performance, especially Shakespeare, includes *Women as Hamlet* (Cambridge University Press).

also available from stork press

Madame Mephisto by A. M. Bakalar
ISBN Paperback: 978-0-9571326-0-3
ISBN eBook: 978-0-9571326-1-0

The Finno-Ugrian Vampire by Noémi Szécsi
Translator: Peter Sherwood
ISBN Paperback: 978-0-9571326-6-5
ISBN eBook: 978-0-9571326-7-2

Freshta by Petra Procházková
Translator: Julia Sherwood
ISBN Paperback: 978-0-9571326-4-1
ISBN eBook: 978-0-9571326-5-8

Illegal Liaisons by Grażyna Plebanek
Translator: Danusia Stok
ISBN Paperback: 978-0-9571326-2-7
ISBN eBook: 978-0-9571326-3-4